MW00440883

Business
Bullseye

www.amplifypublishing.com

For more information, please contact:
Amplify Publishing
620 Herndon Parkway #320
Herndon, VA 20170
info@amplifypublishing.com

Library of Congress Control Number: 2020907166

CPSIA Code: PRFRE1020A
ISBN-13: 978-1-64543-566-2

Printed in Canada

To my wife, Tricia—

For many lifetimes of love and inspiration

Business Bullseye

Take Dead Aim *and* Achieve Great Success

JIM SPURLINO

CONTENTS

BUSINESS BULLSEYE
FROM THE TRENCHES

We all know the adage, "If you fail to plan, you are planning to fail." This makes sense in many cases, but the more important concept, the one that comes *before* the plan, is to identify and know your target. What is the bullseye you are aiming for? Identifying and understanding this is far more important and it should precede any work on planning.

This may seem obvious, but not knowing it often plagues our businesses. It steals precious time and resources from meeting our goals.

In his bestselling book,[1] legendary golf instructor Harvey Penick wrote about the need to "Take Dead Aim." He believed

---

1   Penick, Harvey, and Edwin Shrake. *Harvey Penick's Little Red Book: Lessons and Teachings from a Lifetime in Golf*. Simon & Schuster, 2012.

that when hitting a golf ball, you should focus your mind and all your energy on the intended target. You should not be trying to hit the middle of the fairway or somewhere along the right side of the green. You should pick out your target and Take Dead Aim.

I always thought I was pretty good at this. I prided myself on keeping my managers (and myself) focused on the bullseye, always taking dead aim. Alas, we all forget this important tenet from time to time. A particularly memorable example happened as my team was in the throes of a company unionization effort.

Our Ohio-based company had been expanding and having great success. Business had grown at existing plants in Dayton and Middletown, and we were ready to build new plants in nearby Cincinnati. We studied the market, customers, and key suppliers and identified where to build the first one. In less than a year, it was up and running and we were exceeding sales expectations. Shortly afterwards, we added another plant across town. We felt sure of ourselves and were experiencing a lot of customer support.

Then, we were caught by surprise when the Teamsters Union started efforts to unionize workers at our new plants. Having decertified three unions (including two Teamsters' locals) in the past eight years, I was confident we would repel this movement. I was confident, but perhaps hubris was knocking on my door too.

I met with my management team and went over the plan. We tried to convince employees that they didn't need a union, that we were good guys, and we would treat them well. As this effort wore on, I realized we were losing ground. Worse, we were losing trust and relationships with our employees. I was disappointed in our whole team as we had been working the plan laid out weeks before. Mostly, I was disappointed in myself for misaligning our plan with the bullseye.

We brought in human resource consultants, The Weissman Group, who had an almost perfect record in fighting unionization campaigns across the country. We agreed to gather the team and discuss where we were and what our strategy going forward would be. One Saturday morning, in a conference room at one of our plants (intentionally not the office), we learned a great lesson.

Co-founder Norm Weissman stood at the front of the room after I introduced him. He asked the group what they had been doing and what kind of results they were seeing. The answers varied, including my own, but it all seemed to make sense except the results were lagging.

He stopped the conversation and rolled forward a large whiteboard. It was probably eight feet wide by four feet high. Holding a handful of markers, he walked over to Ed Fulton, one of the operations managers and said, "Ed, take the cap off this marker. I want you to aim and throw it at the board." Ed looked at him for a few seconds and tossed the marker, hitting the board and making a blue mark on the right half of the board. We all looked on, not sure of the point.

Norm walked to the board, inspected the mark, and looked at all of us. "How did Ed do?" We all nodded and said "good." He paused for a minute and surveyed the crowd. He had known us for over a decade and knew we were a smart bunch, highly effective, and productive. He stepped back to the board and turned to us again.

"No, it was not good. In fact, you missed the target and not even close to the bullseye." None of us understood. He continued, "Here is the target and here is the bullseye." As he spoke, he moved to the left side of the board and drew an archery target, with a couple of concentric circles and a bullseye colored in at the center.

He spun around and stared at us. He turned to Ed and asked, "Why didn't you hit the target?" Ed stated the obvious; he had not known where the target was when he threw the marker. Norm nodded and explained what we all then knew but had temporarily forgotten. We can be smart and hardworking and execute our plans perfectly but if we don't know our target, if we are not aiming at the bullseye, then we have little chance in hitting it.

Too often, we confuse visions, missions, goals, and strategy with knowing our bullseye and marshalling all the resources required to focus on hitting it. It is the most important concept to grasp, whether starting a business, growing it, or meeting a challenge. It is always the first concept that needs your attention. And as with many things in business and life, *knowing* your bullseye means understanding it fully as well as your means of hitting it. There are two parts to the equation.

The bullseye itself needs a finite definition, as precise as can be for the type and character of the challenge. Refrain from describing a general target that results in a positive outcome but is possibly of little value. This means the bullseye is defined in your mind and communicated effectively in the minds of your management. Describe it as fully and discretely as possible as well as the outcome of hitting it.

The means of hitting the bullseye are just as important. Just as with archery, knowing the size of the target, the distance to it, the weather conditions, your bow and arrow, and maybe most importantly, your own skill are crucial elements to understand in order to hit the bullseye.

Archery

Let's draw the parallel of my business bullseye and an archery bullseye. Most people are at least familiar with archery or shooting arrows with a bow. Let's look at it in simple terms.

Archery is practiced on a range. A target is set up at one end and the shooter stands at the other. The target is large but has a small circle in the center called the bullseye. There are concentric circles surrounding the bullseye. Points are awarded in descending value from the bullseye to the last circle line. For the purposes of this book, consider that everything inside the outer circle line constitutes the target but that, of course, the bullseye is the most valuable part of the target.

When you set a goal in business, you generally describe it in some way. It may have a maximum or minimum value or sometimes a specific value. The relevant range of positive outcomes is the archery target. The optimal outcome is the bullseye.

The bullseye analogy means the most when discussing a goal and its accompanying strategy and tactics. I push for a definition of the bullseye for a simple reason: I want absolute focus on the optimal outcome without acknowledging there are other acceptable, albeit not as valuable, outcomes. Aiming for the target and *hoping* for the bullseye can breed loss of focus and effort. I never want to stop focusing on the bullseye.

At one end of the archery range is where you stand with your bow and arrows. Consider that there are two factors: 1) you with your current skill and 2) your bow and arrows. In business, this is equivalent to your human and capital resources. In archery, if you are not very good, then you can take lessons and practice. In business, you can hire talent and increase training and education.

In archery, if your bow or arrows are not up to your skill level or affect your ability to hit the target, then you change them for something more suitable. In business, if your manufacturing plant is not suitable or the raw material inputs are unsatisfactory, then you change them for something that is up to the challenge.

The last piece of this analogy has to do with what is in between you and the target. There is space, a certain distance, that must be taken into account. There are the atmosphere and weather conditions, maybe some wind or rain that will affect the flight of your arrows. This could require some adjustment in aim but also might cause you to adjust which bow or arrows you use. There is a lot of interaction and interdependence going on—both with archery and with business.

I'll return to this analogy throughout the book. While the analogy works well, the main focus is going to be discerning the difference between generally aiming at the target versus taking dead aim at the bullseye. Business history is littered with those who generally aim at the target and hit it sometimes, or for a while, before totally missing it altogether. Not as plentiful are the dead-aimers; they are the marksmen, and the most successful in their industry. You will never catch them *not* taking dead aim at the bullseye.

Bullseye vs. Target

I don't want to leave this topic without putting a finer point on what differences sometimes lie between a bullseye and a target. Too often, the definition of "target," as I am using here, means an acceptable range of outcomes. It comes without the precision of a specific target like the term "bullseye." We all know what a bullseye is. It is dead perfect center. It is exactly the right and best outcome. You can't get any better.

A "target," though, can take on some nuances that affect our thinking and, ultimately, our performance. Many of you have experienced the setting of targets in business. There may be sales objectives, quality plans, market penetration goals, et cetera. Many such targets end up being too general or involve some sort of minimum or maximum. While useful in some instances, this often leads to mission-creep as you attempt to hit your real target, the bullseye.

Archery is a clear way to describe the difference between a bullseye and a target, but let's go back to Harvey Penick and golf for a moment. I've played a lot of golf, with a handicap as low as a seven. (For you non-golfers, that's pretty good, better than most amateurs, but still a long way from professionals.) Several times in my life, I've been fortunate enough to play with touring professionals, some of the best golfers in the world. This happened at what's called a Pro-Am event—a round of golf where a pro plays with three or four amateurs the day before a professional tournament starts.

One time, I drew Nancy Lopez, the LPGA legend who has won forty-eight professional tournaments including three majors. Needless to say, I was excited to play alongside the nicest and most engaging professional athlete I have ever met.

On the day of the Pro-Am, I met my playing partners: Nancy, two single digit handicappers, and two high handicappers. Teeing off in front of a crowd *and* Nancy Lopez was nerve wracking! After the first hole jitters and about an hour of playing, we amateurs settled down a bit and I noticed a difference in how the group approached shots.

The high handicappers tended to take aim in very broad terms. Hit the fairway or stay out of the water usually were the extent of their goals. The low handicappers, me included, would take more care. We might aim at the left side of the fairway or the right side of the green. Nancy took dead aim. On every single shot, she had a very specific target, a bullseye, that she aimed for. Whether it was utility pole in the distance or a grain of sand on the green, she had a bullseye as her target. Interestingly, her bullseyes were always two dimensional. There was both direction *and* distance which, as golfers know, are equally important.

I doubt that Nancy's journey of learning golf and improving until she became a professional predates when she started taking dead aim at the bullseye. I suspect she started taking dead aim long before she had the skill to hit bullseyes over and over. It is part and parcel to honing any skill and improving your game.

As in golf (or archery), many of you have experienced setting targets in business. Many such targets end up being too general or involve some sort of minimum or maximum. While useful in some instances, this often leads to mission-creep as you attempt to hit your real target, the bullseye.

My Industry and Background

To give this book some background and color, and to help you understand the jargon I'll be using, I need to describe my own industry and business. My career was in manufacturing and delivering ready-mix concrete, concrete for short. Concrete today is not much different in many ways than when the Romans made it, but it's also dramatically different in other ways. The main ingredients—cement, aggregate, and water—are the same, but those constituents have improved in quality and consistency. In addition, we now have many additives and chemicals we can incorporate with the base product to enhance its performance for any given circumstances. I'm actually selling the changes in our product quite short but that's the basics. A last but most important characteristic of concrete: it is perishable. There is generally a ninety-minute window from the time the mixer truck is loaded to the time it must finish discharging the concrete at a construction site. After that window of time, the product begins to degrade in quality and, ultimately, will become hard and unable to be discharged from the truck. It's a unique wrinkle I'll address in more detail below.

Manufacturing concrete consists of a plant that actually conveys and weighs materials into mixer trucks. These are the trucks you see on the road that have drums or odd-shaped spinning cylinders mounted at an angle to the truck body. A spiral of fins are welded to the inside of the drum. The mixer truck's drum spins and does the mixing (or manufacturing) of the concrete as well as the transportation. The production capacity of a company is the combination of its plants and the number of trucks in use. You can add trucks to increase manufacturing capacity up to the point of the plant's capacity to weigh and load materials into them. Most often, a concrete company's manufacturing capacity is directly related to the number of mixer trucks it owns.

The last piece is the delivery. Contractors buy concrete delivered by mixer trucks to their construction sites. They place orders for delivery at a precise time and at a precise rate. An order might be for one hundred cubic yards delivered at a rate of ten cubic yards every ten minutes to a site that is fifteen miles away. Cubic yards are the unit of measure used to sell concrete, like gallons or pounds. The tricky part is getting delivery right with a perishable product and the unpredictability of traffic problems throughout the day. It is truly a service business, even though it's defined as a manufacturing industry. This is how I came to see and refer to our company as "a service business that just happens to sell concrete."

So, throughout the chapters, I hope not to overuse jargon, but you may run into concrete, cubic yards, plants, trucks or mixers, contractors, and so on. Just fair warning.

I don't want to leave this section without one other comment. Every businessperson I meet talks about how competitive or difficult their industry is. I am the same way. When someone inevitably asks what the concrete industry is like, I describe it as being like air traffic control. At the beginning of the day, our plan is perfectly laid out. We know exactly which orders start when and where they go. We plan to shuttle trucks to different plants based on demand and supply and then shuttle them back to other destinations. It can all be logically and perfectly laid out.

Then the day begins, and your plan all goes to hell, virtually every day. Traffic back-ups, accidents, truck maintenance issues, weather issues, customers changing orders, and everything else you can think of happen regularly. Like commercial flying, it is a perfectly laid-out schedule, a dance that could be performed without any hitches, but only in a vacuum. So, we are just like air traffic control but remember to throw in the variable that air traffic control doesn't have to deal with: our perishable product. If we get delayed by traffic or accidents, our product may deteriorate to the point that it is not acceptable for use.

Whether or not you have the skill set to hit a bullseye, never let your aim focus on a general target. The resources, time, and effort that it takes to hit a general target, a fairway, or the middle of green are often the same as the perfect spot, a bullseye.

It's the same in business. The best outcomes will come from

aiming at the bullseye. The more you aim at it, the more often you will hit it. Otherwise, you would have to believe that luck overcomes and outperforms skill. Consider also that waste, inefficiency, and even failure come from not taking dead aim at the bullseye. In golf, if I aim at the bullseye and hit ten yards to the left, that's probably an acceptable outcome. If I aim at a general target and hit ten yards to the left, I may be out of bounds and incur a penalty. Take dead aim at the bullseye and begin to reap the rewards.

CHAPTER 1

KNOWING YOUR BUSINESS INSIDE AND OUT

Knowing your business and your industry inside and out is a prerequisite for success. It is not enough to be proficient at business in general or an expert at your product and services. It requires a complete knowledge of both. Starting and running your own business is fraught with enough challenges. You don't need the additional handicap of not being knowledgeable about the entire landscape of your business and industry.

Three-Legged Stool

There are three components that form a stable foundation of knowledge that are just like a three-legged stool. A deficiency or lack of any one leg will cause your balance to be off or even fall apart. The first is a solid formal education. For me, that meant a bachelor's degree and an MBA. Many of us question the value of what we were learning while in college. Mediocre professors and concepts that seemed dated or irrelevant were often our complaints in undergraduate school. Graduate school was an improvement, but there was still a nagging feeling that the content was not always what we'd use in the future. Years later, I have changed my mind. I am not alone. I have never met a single person in business who regretted getting a college degree. Business owners are particularly adamant that their college degrees were invaluable throughout their career.

The second leg is industry knowledge—about knowing your products and services. It's about knowing how customers and suppliers function in your market. It is all the ins and outs of what make successful companies thrive in your industry. This knowledge is critical to identifying future opportunities and threats and building a sustainable enterprise. Sometimes, this can be attained through education and training, but often is acquired through hard work and engagement in the industry. Learning from others is key to this, but it is also reliant on seeking it out for oneself. It doesn't often get dropped in your lap.

Early on, to make a living and pay for college, I went to work for a privately owned, ready-mix concrete company. I ended up staying in that business for fifteen years and rose through the ranks to eventually be vice president and general manager. I held virtually every job in the company and knew the demands and challenges of each position. I also developed a keen understanding of how and why we were successful and when we were not. This critical and invaluable experience, combined with my college education, gave me the advantage I needed when starting my own business. I cannot imagine my business's early successes without both.

The third leg is gaining knowledge of your own company, its strengths and weaknesses, and how best to maximize your potential by applying the resources you have. It is like the self-actualization part of Maslow's Hierarchy of Needs. It is where the rubber meets the road, the best and most rewarding part of owning and running your own company. The strategic plans and decisions made when combining all three bases of knowledge are the true definition of synergy. Knowledge and experience meet application and execution and provide the impetus for success. My own experience with this was palpable.

> In the year 2000, the country was coming off a long economic expansion and still running strong. I was able to borrow almost $10 million to purchase the capital equipment and get a line of credit to start my own concrete company. My total cash investment was only $40,000, but I also had to take on some minority partners to guarantee the rest of the debt.
>
> Starting my own company was the most exhilarating thing I've ever done professionally. I am also not sure I'd do it again. There were endless days and nights putting together a business plan, negotiating with banks and suppliers, recruiting employees, and talking to future customers. It was exciting but also like being the engineer of a speeding locomotive headed for a dark tunnel with no knowledge of what lay on the other side. I was confident we had the right plan and had done our homework, but you never know until you start heading down the track.
>
> We made it through the tunnel and while the business had its ups and down, we persevered and were profitable in

the first full year. We remained profitable every year except two during the recession when we lost a small amount. That was also the two years when I started telling our bankers that at least we were "cash flow positive" instead of referring to profitability! It was not much fun, but we made it through that period too.

After seventeen years, I came to a strategic crossroads. Our business was very profitable and stable, but the industry was experiencing yet another wave of consolidation. When a major acquisition in our market became available, I was excited at the opportunity but lost a bidding war to another company. The triumphant party from the war approached me and I sold out less than a year later to them.

It was bittersweet. Starting and owning my own company was a dream and a joy most days, but the offer I received was priced at a multiple of earnings that was well above the market. Now I knew why I lost the bidding war!

In addition to the importance of the three-legged stool of knowledge, there is always a need to remain a lifelong learner. None of us will ever know it all. Continuing to learn throughout a career keeps our minds sharp as we navigate the always changing landscape of our businesses. I was never passionate about continuing education, but I always seemed to find ways to incorporate extra learning into every year.

Everyone Needs Help

Related to this is the difficulty of bringing in high-level, C-suite caliber talent to help run a small- or medium-sized business.

Usually, it's a budget constraint. Smaller businesses just can't afford the talent they may need. It's a common bit of "chicken and egg" problem-solving. This challenge forced me to take on more responsibilities for strategic issues and long-term planning. In turn, this also meant that my knowledge and experience had to be augmented with a wide variety of subject matter.

Several years ago, after I became friends with a CEO of a very large company in our industry, he asked, "Who do you talk to about big issues? Who helps you decide what course to pursue?" In fact, he was asking me who helped define our goals and strategies. It is an ongoing challenge many of us face with little or no help from our own management. I found several ways to try to overcome or at least compensate for this situation.

In 1996, former Iams pet food executive Clay Mathile founded Aileron, an organization for the education of entrepreneurs. He did so shortly after selling his company to Procter & Gamble, becoming Dayton, Ohio's, only billionaire. Clay's story is a great one. He rose through the ranks of Iams, as the pet food industry had taken off with new variants of premium offerings, eventually becoming CEO. One of his gifts back to the Dayton community, and to entrepreneurs in general, was a non-profit whose mission is to serve the needs of small and medium companies. Aileron offers courses and other assistance to CEOs and their senior management on a variety of management topics.

Several years ago, I took Aileron's two-day course for CEOs. It was meant particularly for individuals that might not have much C-suite or general management experience and whose companies were often in their first years of existence. Although the course was mostly too basic for my education and experience, I found two valuable rec-ommendations.

The first involved growth prospects. I have modified and used it periodically ever since. The exercise is to evaluate your key management team for their ability to grow with your company. Essentially, it amounted to a spreadsheet I developed for each key member of my management team, identifying their strengths, weaknesses, needs (education and training), overall current rating, and future potential. The goal was to identify who could take on more responsibility or move up into the next higher position and who might hold us back. The first time I used it, the results were eye-opening.

Most of my management team were very strong per-formers with few weaknesses in their current position. However, none of them were capable of the next level. It was not that they had liabilities in any way; it was that they simply could not fill the next position up if we grew signifi-cantly. For example, my Controller could not be a CFO, my Sales Manager could not be a VP of Sales, and my strongest Operations Manger could not be a COO. All of them were great individuals, but we were not going to grow significantly without bringing new people in.

In many ways, this exercise kept me on the lookout for quality individuals and the possibility of adding to my team. Corporate growth is rarely a smooth upward trend but almost always in fits and starts with occasional setbacks. Adding to your manage-ment team will probably look the same. It will be stairstep in nature, meaning you constantly will go from being somewhat over-staffed to somewhat under-staffed. For example, if you are in slow growth mode, you might hire and/or promote slowly over time, alternatively having just enough senior management and then occasionally a bit extra when you find a particularly valuable person prior to an actual need. In a faster growth environment, this is accelerated to alternating more often and in bigger steps. Think of it as always staying ahead; it's a matter of how far, which is dependent on your rate of growth. Of course, big acquisitions can throw all this out the door temporarily.

The last point on this exercise, and another modification I added, was to include myself in the analysis. It was a difficult task. There are outside tools to assist you, such as aptitude tests and 360-degree evaluations, but just objectively assessing your own capacity can be helpful. Many small-company CEOs tend to take on all or part of other C-suite roles such as CFO or COO. When growth opportunities come, especially significant or sustained growth, they are often accompanied by hard decisions for the CEO to let go of an area of responsibility and bring in talent to replace part of their workload. An honest self-evaluation will help lead you to difficult but critical decisions.

The other recommendation I found interesting but did not take was to form a board of directors or advisors. Such a board would have regular meetings and give input that would be taken honestly and seriously. I had never taken this formal step before and was reluctant to do so. Academically, it made sense, but I had reservations. I had seen other companies our size form boards, but no matter what the intent, they wound up being less than effective or not independent. It often ended up consisting of their accountant, their attorney, their retired friend, et cetera, and it never worked out. Also, I hesitated to give up the speed at which I operated and prided our company on. We were a finely tuned sports car and highly maneuverable on a moment's notice. I did not want to jeopardize that agility. Finally, and selfishly, I did not want to spend the time getting individual board members up to speed on our business and then keeping them there.

Of course, all these things can be overcome and are not good reasons to forgo the advantages of outside advisors. They are probably closer to excuses than reasons. While I never reconciled my view of the costs versus benefits and therefore never had a board, I think I found a better fit for me and possibly others. That's described in the next story.

Overall, Aileron helped fill one of my needs for continuing my education. It helped me look at my own company in new and different ways and apply this knowledge. It also reminded me to spend more time working *on* my business rather than *in* my business. Another learning opportunity helped me understand more about the industry we operated in and offered insights I would not have found anywhere else.

Shortly after attending Aileron, I joined a peer group. Generically, a peer group is like it sounds: a group of comparably positioned leaders and decision makers that meet regularly to discuss their businesses. For many, this can function like a best practices group, a consulting team, or sometimes like a board. Such peer groups exist in many industries although finding them may require effort. They include groups like Young Presidents Organization (YPO) or Vistage, which offer groups that are geographically organized but not by industry. Both have existed for many years. Because I knew many participants that spoke highly of their time in such settings, I came close to joining a YPO group but stopped short when I found a better alternative.

The peer group I joined was one of two being run by a large consulting company in our industry. Each had between seven and nine members, all at the CEO/President/C-suite level of their company. Members were from across the country but had essentially the same job in the same industry. They were chosen carefully, never from competing companies, and tried to fit the right personalities together. I was fortunate to know two of the members beforehand and immediately clicked with the others.

While not run exactly like a board meeting, the peer group met twice a year for two days each. During the meeting, every company CEO had time to review their company and get feedback as well as talk about industry issues and general trends.

It is remarkable that in such a short time, about a year, you have a group of peers that know you and your company, can give valuable advice and, what I found most beneficial, hold you accountable. That is, if I had presented information or forecasts or plans of action in prior meetings, they would hold me accountable for results at the next meeting. With these peers, there was no holding back or excuses. It was unique because we were all equals, participating and reciprocating with quality time and advice. It was an invaluable experience, and I never left a meeting thinking it was a waste of time or that they didn't understand a situation. I always left with new ideas, new plans, or the promise to revisit a strategy that my peer group had criticized (usually rightfully so).

Both Aileron and my peer group emphasized critical analysis of my most valuable resource: my own management team. This was one of the most relevant steps in deciding what strategic direction to take my company. While it is always an option to bring in new team members just when new growth opportunities arise, it is also a risk if they do not understand or embrace your culture. My Achilles' heel was in hesitating to bring on new talent into senior management. I often erred on keeping costs low when, in retrospect, that decision cost us potential growth in the long term. Be cautious about overspending but don't try and save a dime when dollars are in front of you. Understanding your own team and developing a plan to strengthen it will pay big dividends.

Analyzing your team's potential and capacity is important, but being able to get educated and insightful feedback and advice is also critical for any CEO. My decision to pursue a peer group was based on my own views of what my company and I needed and the quality of the group itself. If the peer group was not providing value, I likely would have wound up with a board. It was simply a matter of finding the right avenue for me and, most importantly, finding feedback and advice that brought value to the company.

Speed and Agility

Knowing your business inside and out and continuing to learn throughout your career contribute significantly to the speed and agility with which your business can take strategic action. If action does not follow shortly after attaining critical new information, it will affect efficiency, profitability, or even overall success. I prided myself and my company on our ability to recognize opportunities and threats and change our aim or bullseyes quickly. It may seem reactionary, but that is not as bad as some would have you believe. Often you need to react to changing environments and conditions that affect hitting a bullseye. Not doing so can be detrimental or even deadly to your business. Here is an example.

In the early 2000s, the Department of Justice conducted an investigation into price-fixing by Indianapolis-area concrete producers. They found that several firms and some of their leaders—representing most of the production capacity in the market—were guilty of price-fixing. There would be record fines and many owners and senior managers going to jail. Customers expressed outrage and anger at these companies. We saw an opportunity to enter the market and take advantage of this sentiment.

In 2005, we purchased a small business in the market—one that was not involved in the scandal. We also secured a very large, high-profile construction project, the Lucas Oil Stadium, home of the Indianapolis Colts. It seemed like a perfect entry into a new market. For the first few years, things went well as we successfully completed the project and went on to supply the new convention center as well. We increased sales by 50 percent in the first twenty-four months and were immediately profitable. Our bullseye was to become the second largest company in the market in five years and we seemed well on the way to it.

By our third year doing business in Indianapolis, I began to see signs of weaker sales and lower prices, and our internal forecasts did not indicate that would change. I was receiving and processing information regularly. We continued to adjust our strategy, still seeking the same bullseye. By year four and five, the only thing that had changed was an increased rate of deterioration in the market. We were faced with a looming recession, falling prices, and a management team there that was forever optimistic (and, unfortunately, me buying it).

We rode through the recession with a string of up-and-down years. Each up-year brought a sliver of hope that we were back on plan—only to be dashed by the following year. It was torture. I had abandoned the goal of being #2 in the market and hoped just to salvage our investment. The only exit plan was liquidation, since no buyers were in the market for a small, failing operation in Indianapolis.

The recession eventually ended—slowly and without real growth. There was significant consolidation in the market that allowed margins to rise and we recovered enough to be slightly profitable. The problem was, we had dug a hole in five years that would take fifteen years to get out of.

In retrospect, we failed to realize that our original and only bullseye quickly became unattainable and irrelevant. We received information in a timely fashion, but our analysis was flawed as we continued to only adjust strategy. We never adjusted the bullseye or created an intermediate bullseye that would have allowed us to exit early. When we eventually sold the business, we recouped our original investment and then some, but the sale proceeds did not approach our accumulated total losses. Our mistakes cost us not only money but a drain on resources and management attention. Because of the drain, we also lost out on other multiple opportunities we could have pursued as we struggled through this time.

Consider setting up intermediate checkpoints on your way to the bullseye. They should include milestones that are specific with an understanding of consequences for failing to meet each. For example, this could be go/no-go junctures, an aggregation of factors, or a sequence of factors that determine whether to proceed, adjust strategy, or adjust the bullseye. And, trust what your eyes are telling you. If the information you are receiving indicates a new strategy is needed or even if the pursuit should be called off, then trust that information and act on it in a timely fashion. Nothing is more deadly than inaction or paralysis in the face of mounting evidence.

CHAPTER 2

CREATING THE IDEAL CULTURE

Culture may be the least understood and most important concept determining the success of your company. Definitions and components may vary but at its core, culture is about a company's values and beliefs and, here's the important part, it's also how they are put into action. Communicating culture is only effective when there is evidence that leadership believes in that culture—and continually executes its business every day according to it.

As CEO, I was the chief caretaker of our culture. I often repeated our mantras and the stories that illustrated them. Culture must live and breathe from top to bottom if you want to hit your bullseye. For instance, in our very first year in business, my management team understood what I had said about customer service goals. They knew the words I spoke and understood the bullseye I was describing. They could repeat it back and give hypothetical examples. However, actions and real-life stories often underscore concepts in a powerful and memorable way that words alone cannot.

Culture Gets Created

Given the importance of culture to my company, I always was on the lookout for ways to reinforce it. Leading by example is the best way. In our first few months in business, we had secured a large rest area project on Interstate 75 north of Cincinnati. Our customer, Complete Concrete, was the largest concrete contractor in the U.S. While I had known Complete for some time, and believed they respected me, I knew this was a huge test for my new company.

We started the project in mid-summer, with some of the biggest product delivery days still ahead of us. As summer gave way to fall, opportunities for these big delivery days dwindled because of the weather. One Saturday morning, I got a call from Lewis Mander, one of their vice presidents. He told me that the weather forecast had changed, and it looked like rain all the following week. To keep on schedule, they had one large placement of product they were anxious to do, and it looked like today—the day he called—was the only day in the next seven days that weather would permit it. I cringed as he asked the question I knew was coming. Is there any way we could do it today?

I looked at my watch and said yes. I also asked for an hour to figure out logistics and get back to him on when we could start. I had to find thirty employees and get raw materials delivered to our plant, all on a Saturday that we were not expecting to work, and with no one at our facilities.

I called my two operations managers and started a chain of phone calls. It would require getting 60 percent of our entire new workforce to stop what they were doing on a Saturday and come to work. It also meant that four different raw material suppliers would get the same request. We would need approximately fifty-five semi-truck load deliveries from them in order to process the order. I called Lewis for a little more time.

An hour and a half later, we had confirmation that we could get the needed supplies and had rounded up almost all the thirty employees needed. I called Lewis again and let him know we could start just before noon. He sounded elated and I headed to the plant.

As the employees started to roll in, I had one thing in mind: Thank every one of them for giving up a Saturday afternoon on short notice and giving us a chance to WOW a customer. As the trucks fired up and began loading concrete, I radioed our sales manager who was on the project site and let him know we had started. He would be spending his Saturday directing traffic for our trucks on a busy interstate.

To run a concrete plant, it can take as few as two people: one person at the computer controls of the plant and another running a big Caterpillar loader that feeds raw materials into the plant. I was standing in the control room of the plant watching trucks get loaded and heading out of the gate. Our regular Plant Manager, Dave, was at the controls and my Operations Manager, Lou, walked in from running the loader. We had successfully loaded the first of many rounds for our trucks and there was a slight break while waiting for the first trucks to return for their next load.

Looking at our truck yard, I saw one truck left in the parking lot. I asked Lou who was going to drive it. He said that everyone who could come in was already here and loaded and it was an extra truck. I said, "Well, there are three of us and we only need two at the plant. Let's flip coins; odd man out drives the last truck." They knew that I could do a passible job of any of the three tasks, but the offer seemed to shock them a bit. Lou volunteered to drive and said I could run the loader—the easier of the three jobs. I said no and pulled a coin out of my pocket and looked at them both. I said, "Come on, let's go," and they slowly found a coin themselves, and we all flipped at once. I came up heads. The only heads that came up. I was the odd man out.

Lou again tried to convince me to run the loader, but I had grabbed the truck keys and was on my way out the door. I jumped into the truck and started it up. My pulse was getting faster. I pulled the truck under the loading area for my first load. To be honest, it had been many years since I had driven a fully loaded truck, and these trucks are some of the most top-heavy, demanding vehicles to drive on the road. I was nervous but excited.

As I approached the site, my Sales Manager was waving his arms at the top of the exit ramp. I stopped and he looked like a kid with a new toy. "I can't believe you're doing this! This is amazing! All the Complete guys know it's you. This is so cool!"

I eased down the ramp and began to maneuver the truck to where it would unload. A Complete employee was directing as I backed up and started to unload. I made a few minor mistakes that took extra time but provided some levity for the Complete crew. I was soon unloaded and headed back to the plant for another load. We worked for over ten hours that day to get the customer what they wanted—and did it in spades.

The next Monday, Lewis called to thank me. He said we did a great job. He was particularly grateful for even considering, let alone fulfilling, his last-minute, weekend request. He said he did not expect any of our competitors would have even contemplated it. Before we hung up, he said, "One last thing. I heard about you driving the last truck. My guys couldn't believe it and frankly I can't either. That says *a lot*. I can't tell you how much I appreciate everything. You will definitely be seeing more work from Complete."

Over the years, I have continued to hear Lewis and many of his employees tell that story. It made a lasting impression—and a statement about how my company felt about customer service. Just as important, the story became a pillar for our employees about our culture. It was retold countless times. To truly hit a cultural bullseye, it's important to be able to articulate what you want, but actions and the stories that emanate from them will live for many years. When behaviors back up the talk, then this type of bullseye gets hit square in the center.

From the beginning of my company's existence, we set out to define a new level of customer service in our market. To that end, we start as every company does by stating our beliefs regarding customers and how we want to treat them. Overall, everyone in the company knew we considered ourselves a "service business that just happens to sell concrete," but we added a simple mantra. It's an adage with a twist: "If a customer makes a request, the answer is Yes!" Then we added, "Unless it is immoral, illegal, unethical, or unsafe." Note that it doesn't say anything about price, just our willingness to do anything to help our customer. Anyone in the company was authorized to say "yes," but only the Sales Department was authorized to price it.

This adage worked because it is simple and doesn't judge the customer nor impose rules or limitations that only suit us. It also was successful because we worked hard on our culture. It is easy to refer to corporate values or mission or vision statements, but the truth is that most employees can't recite all or even any of them. What all employees can do is *tell* you about the company and what comes out is the culture. And the most effective way to convey your culture, the values and behaviors that you want embraced, is to tell stories. Here are a couple of customer service—I mean *culture* stories.

Culture in Action

Ronnie O'Rourke was one of my salesmen, but his background had been in operations. He understood operating plants and quality control but had not had a lot experience in selling to or dealing with customers. I remember explaining to him that he *did* understand customers because he was one, every day, and many times a day. I gave him the simple advice that he just needed to put himself in their shoes and help solve their problems. Off he went into the world of sales.

Ronnie had worked with us long enough to understand our culture when it came to customer service, but he surprised me a few months later. He had called on a customer that had been frustrating him for some time. The customer never seemed to have time for Ronnie, and we were not selling him anything. Ronnie found him on a construction site with his surveying equipment. He was laying out a new building. When Ronnie approached him, he said he didn't have time to talk because he needed to finish laying out the building's foundation for the next day's work and didn't have any help with him. (Surveying requires at least two people. If you are alone, the work is almost impossible, but this guy was doing it.)

Ronnie asked again if he had just a few minutes—to which he replied that the only way would be if Ronnie wanted to help him finish surveying the site. I'm sure he expected that would be the end of the conversation, but Ronnie immediately said, "Okay, tell me what you want me to do." He then spent the next three hours helping finish the work. He'd stand with the tall stick where the customer told him to, moving all over the site until they were done. Wiping his brow but with a smile on his face, he thanked Ronnie and said, "Come to my office tomorrow at 7 AM and we will talk." We took over all his work the next day.

Early on, we had one of our largest customers schedule the biggest day of product deliveries in our short history. Eighteen of our trucks were scheduled to begin deliveries at 6 AM and each truck would make several roundtrips. The timing and consistency of deliveries was very important. As the first several trucks began arriving at the construction site, they noticed the entrance was blocked by pallets of steel delivered by another company. The first driver notified the customer's foreman and was told he would have to wait until he freed up a forklift. By the look of things, the first driver knew it would take a while and affect not just our efficiency but also the customer—even though it was their own doing.

More drivers joined the first and looked on. Before the foreman could walk away, the first driver asked where the steel needed to be moved. He was pointed in a direction and said the forklift would be a while, but they were hurrying the best they could. As he turned to walk away, he groused that his boss would be upset with him for the delay. With that, the drivers looked at each other, nodded, and then went over to the pallets of steel and began to move them, one piece at a time. It was hard work and tedious. Rather than a forklift moving several pallets in fifteen minutes, this took almost an hour of strenuous manual effort to do piece by piece and then assemble everything back on the pallets.

When the drivers were done, out of breath and sweating though their clothes, they jumped in their trucks and drove into the site. On a call later that morning, I don't think I've ever heard a more grateful foreman. Our drivers had saved him delay time but also saved our company time and money. Everyone won and we had another customer for life.

These two stories have some important things in common. They were typical of the way we communicated culture. We had a printed statement about customer service, but it wasn't always a clean and concise statement or definition that communicated effectively. What worked was the statement backed up with the stories. The stories gave color, texture, and commitment to what we printed. No one could be confused about those messages. We reinforced it with the way we talked and *acted*, driving it deep into our culture.

Culture Differences

Culture can be a philosophical topic but always must be held true by the company's leadership. Over the years, I have had numerous conversations with CEOs about how companies are led and managed. It often wound up being informative but not applicable. Debating subjects that deal with culture can often find two like-minded people differing significantly. While the bullseye can be the same, the experiences and thought processes can vary wildly. There can always be more than one right answer, and different means to an end, but the ability to absorb information can become clouded by experiences that bias sound thinking. You can't hit the bullseye by constantly thinking in your own experiences and disregarding others. You are not always right. Here's what I'm talking about:

Carl Stovall is a legend among legends in our industry. This remarkable man started constructing concrete sidewalks in a small town in Ohio as a teenager and has grown to become one of the largest concrete contractors in the U.S.

While I had known Carl for years, we became friends when I started my own company. He had known and done business with my dad. When I started my company, he was generous and receptive to talking to me and eventually we became good personal friends. We spent personal time together, dinners and vacations, but still often and almost always returned to talking business. I valued his opinions greatly and, I think, he came to value mine equally as well.

Our friendship was an achievement itself given that we didn't think alike on many subjects. I consider that a testament to both our open-mindedness and willingness, almost a yearning, to learn. Although Carl never graduated from college and I had an MBA, you would never have known that unless you asked. He was as learned as any Ivy League business scholar. From all he taught me, he stands out as an exception to my thoughts on education for business leaders.

Our biggest departure in business philosophy always came in how we led our senior management teams and, as importantly, how that culture was infused down throughout our respective managers and businesses.

Carl was highly competitive. He grew up in a large family that struggled financially but had a great core, especially in his mom. The kids were often left to fend for themselves; clearly Carl excelled at the challenge. He worked harder than anyone else and was always open to learning more. This compelled him to be the success he is today and to let his competitive spirit permeate through his company culture. Everyone is always competing at his company and he believes that competitive environment drives performance.

Carl's philosophy may work if done in doses and with the right structure. However, I don't naturally embrace it; my own experience says otherwise. I always drove my company's competitive energy outside the company, towards customers and competitors. I drove my team to beat other teams. He drove his individuals to be their best and hopefully, collectively, beat other teams.

I also grew up in a large family and had a great a core in my mom. We were better off financially than Carl's family but still often left to figure out our own paths to the future as well. I don't believe that Carl and I embraced dramatically different values as we grew up but rather evolved differently from our experiences.

Early on, my experiences led to believing that everyone

around me had to succeed for me to succeed. This applied to everyone including those outside my family or close friends. Later, in business, this formed the basis of competing as a team against our competitors or others not aligned with our goals. I'm not sure where this wiring came from but absolutely believe that our success was based upon something larger than myself.

The big difference between Carl and me is that he believed in the internal competition among his managers to drive greater performance, and even perpetual improvement. I believed in external competition as in "us versus them." We only competed against our market competition, so we either won or lost together. These philosophies are not mutually exclusive, but by nature, employees tend to focus on "me" first, then "us" in business. It's human nature. So, if there is additional focus put on the *me* from leadership, then I believe the *us* gets lost—or at best takes a back seat.

Another significant difference is that of managing in real time versus emphasizing past results. We need to understand past results to gain insight and improve, but overemphasizing past results will take away time and resources from focusing on the future. Both are important but balance is good. After a performance review, I often made sure there was a clear understanding of the past but always put the emphasis squarely on the future. There's a reason why the windshield in your car is many times larger than the rear-view mirror.

Competition can be a great motivator and driver of performance but it can also be a detriment to the overall goal. Most sports have this delineation. They are either individual or team sports but rarely crossover. In golf, the difference between every other tournament and the Ryder Cup is huge. In a typical tournament, you want to beat everyone else. This happens every week except for the Ryder Cup. Then, you want your team to beat the other team. And you cheer on the same teammate that week that you want to beat the crap out of for the rest of the year.

Shouldn't it Be *We*?

In my own company, I trained myself and made it a habit always to say "we" and "our." It became second nature. Even though my name was on the side of every truck and every plant my company owned, I never let myself fall into the trap of saying "I," "my," or "mine." Some of this came from my previous employer saying "my trucks" or "my company" and seeing employees recoil. I wanted everyone to know I considered the company "ours" and its success was based on everyone's involvement. We succeeded or failed together.

It may seem like a small thing—just words. And of course, every employee knew that I owned the company and that the trucks and plants were mine. However, for me to act like we were "we" made a big difference. My senior managers have commented on this, complimenting me on always saying "we" and how it made them feel and how it made everyone that worked for us feel. This part of our culture meant that WE had common focus and interest and were determined to succeed for all of us. Here are two contrasting stories that Carl Stovall and I told each other one evening.

Carl recounted the difficulty of having multiple divisions, led by different leaders, that occasionally need to help each other out. His Eastern Division had obtained a large, difficult project and was struggling to keep on schedule. This meant extra costs in labor and materials to catch up and therefore a threat that they would lose money on this project. He knew it was management that was the problem on this project.

I knew Carl's company had several very qualified managers for this type of project and asked why he didn't just send in his best to straighten things out. This is where the story became strange to me. Carl said he did just that. He had called his Western Division VP and told him to send help to the Eastern Division project. It just did not go as planned. "Well," he said, "what happens is Bobby ends up sending his 'C' team to help. Then, Albert complains that the project is doing worse because of the lousy guys Bobby sent. There's back and forth: his guys make more, their guys aren't listening, blah, blah, blah."

I had one question, "Why not just tell Bobby to send someone better?" The answer was the root cause of the problem to me. Carl explained that his culture was such that these divisions, and therefore the VPs, competed against each other—for biggest project, most sales, most profit . . . everything! In fact, a significant percentage of their compensation was based on division profits. So, to send quality management to help another division out would only hurt that division VP. His projects and even his own pocketbook would suffer. This, in fact, often happened within divisions as well, since project managers were treated the same way.

I had no doubt that Carl believed in setting up a competitive nature in his culture, but I could not understand how it benefited his company. There were huge impediments set up to keep his key managers from doing what was best for the company. There was also plenty of motivation for his managers to act in their own best interest, even when it was detrimental to the company as a whole.

In contrast, "we" prevented this from ever happening at my company (Yes, I know. I should have said "our" company.) Here is the contrasting story I told Carl after hashing out all the details of his experience with Bobby and Albert and their divisional battles.

Lou, my most experienced operations manager, called me early one morning. He was letting me know what he was doing that day. He wasn't asking and he wasn't unsure of the right thing to do. He was just letting me know.

"Morning Jim. Just wanted you to know I'm headed over to Indy for the day. Jeff has a big order on downtown and another order at the north plant at the same time. The plant manager at the north plant is on vacation this week and sounded like he needed some help pretty bad. I told him I'd handle north, and he can stay downtown." None of this surprised me. In fact, there are hundreds of such instances. He continued, "Oh yeah, and we aren't too busy today at my plants, so pretty sure all is handled there by my guys. Need anything from me?"

I never thought twice about this call or other ones like it. My management knew that I expected them to do what was best for the company. Period. Lou was typically responsible for the plants operating in the north part of our Ohio market. He was never responsible for anything in Indianapolis. What I especially appreciated was that I didn't even become involved in most of these situations. My managers talked to each other regularly, shared equipment, shared people, and shared themselves like it was second nature—because that was our culture. It was imbedded in our work DNA. We would all succeed or fail together but it would always be together. That is how "we" were.

In our effort to hit a bullseye, we do everyone a disservice by not cheering on the team every week. Competition can be good but only when it inspires *and* informs others. It is counterproductive when winners tear down losers within the same company. In hunting bullseyes, competition should be a brotherhood and not an adversary environment. I'm happy to applaud organizations that have found a way to make competition a beneficial element in their culture—but only if it generates idea-sharing, support, cooperation, and genuine concern for others and the business overall. If not, even the apparent benefits may be outweighed by the costs. In any case, they are not sustainable.

CHAPTER 3

PARTNERS—THEY'RE GOOD FOR ONLY ONE THING

I will not make you wait. What is the "one thing" partners are good for? I learned what it was from Dave, my attorney. We were discussing the end of particularly bad partnership episode I went through when he told me of a client of his. He described him as a real estate developer and successful businessman in town. He said that, after quite a few partners in different deals, he had come to a realization. The client said, "Dave, you know what the only thing partners are good for?" Dave said no and he replied "F#CK!@G!" I'm not sure which side of the equation he was on, but I know what he means.

I will not pretend to think there are many good reasons to have a partner. My experience is succinct—that it is almost always a bad idea except under a few circumstances. Even then, there are risks. In other words, the default ought to be *not* to have partners unless unusual circumstances make it obvious. (I'll get back to this at the end of this chapter.)

People consider having a partner most often for three reasons. The first and foremost is money. A partner may have money or be able to bring it in. If that's your reason, I'd suggest trying harder to borrow it. The terms and conditions may seem onerous, but a partner can bring a ton of mischief later. The second is time. There doesn't seem like enough time to wait and this partner-to-be is standing in front of me. If that's your reason, I'd suggest a little patience. You will kill to get this time back when confronted with partner issues later. The third is more nebulous. It is out of the desire to do this new venture with someone. You don't want to do it alone and doing it with someone is safer and more comfortable. If that's your reason, follow the saying about wanting a friend in Washington, DC: "Get a dog." Don't let this desire lull you into a partnership.

While this might seem cynical, I am serious about cautioning anyone to slowly, strongly, and carefully consider all options before taking on a partner. My worst experience began when I started my own company and didn't end until ten years later.

The Worst

Starting my first major business was the epitome of a new and challenging bullseye. I had just ended fifteen years of employment with a company and found myself ready to start my own business. It would be in the same industry and geographic area as my previous employer, which represented advantages as well as challenges. I had several major concerns—all of them go/no-go decisions.

The first was financing. My plan was to greenfield three plants and all their associated equipment. My analysis was that this would be approximately $8 million in capital expenditures and another $2 million in a line of credit. Over fifteen years of employment, I had risen to vice president and general manager of one of the largest companies in our industry in Ohio. I also handled much of the banking for the company and so I had developed relationships with many of the banks in our area. (To top it off, it was the year 2000, when banks actually loaned money!)

I had written a complete and compelling business plan and presented it to several banks. The fact that I had developed these relationships and built my reputation over the years was of immense value. Though there was real interest from a few of them, it was obvious that I needed help in the form of paid-in capital or strong debt guarantors. I canvassed my friends and began conversations to take on partners.

Several were interested and willing to make a small cash investment and then sign on to guarantee the debt. There were four partners in all, but my equity had shrunk to just over 50 percent. It was my minimum threshold if they would agree to my attorney's operating agreement, the legal agreement stating how the company is run and who has authority for certain issues. They agreed and we were off.

My business got started successfully and we were profitable in our first full year. We also were hitting or exceeding all the forecasts in the business plan. This was a surprise to the bankers who told me later that they assume all entrepreneurs are way too optimistic in their forecasts! Over time, the business continued to grow and remain profitable but my relationship with one partner soured for personal reasons. He was the type of partner who seemed to think it was his company and he deserved something more than he was entitled to. I generally ignored him and thought he would either come to his senses or at least stop his detrimental behavior.

I was wrong. He came in one day and demanded more information than we had and then access to ten years of records for his own accountants to review. He wanted the records provided by my staff and their cooperation with his accountants while they took up our conference room for weeks. I told him we would provide any information we possess but that we couldn't afford to tie up the business' accounting staff or our only conference room for multiple weeks. Although he had been provided an independent accounting firm's audited financial statements since the beginning, it did not sit well with him. Within weeks he filed a lawsuit.

Over the next two years, we spent time on discovery, document production, depositions, and, of course, legal fees. It ended up in a trial where his side put on a week's worth of testimony and evidence. At the end of the week, our attorney had filed a dismissal motion that was granted. His lead and only expert witness had almost all his work and testimony thrown out and his case was left in shambles. We were to put on our case for damages the following week. I was confident we would win.

The weekend saw a flurry of calls from his attorney attempting to settle the matter. I refused. Being confident and pissed off are a strong combination. On Monday, we began our case for damages. It was not going well for him. At the morning break, his attorney once again pressed for a settlement. Their offer was getting significantly better. I was still adamant about pursuing our damages, but my attorneys sensed a good deal. My intention was to exact a pound of flesh and my judgment was likely skewed in the heat of the battle. Finally, the lead attorney asked that I talk to the lead co-counsel. He spoke quietly and convincingly about his rationale for taking the settlement. In the end, I knew to trust him and agreed to the settlement albeit still cranky about it. It left the soon-to-be ex-partner without ownership in the company and took his ownership from another entity we held together for a small sum. I knew we had won a huge victory for a very small price. Or did we?

While the settlement was very favorable, and he was out of my life, it had taken two years. It was a big distraction. The other partners had been bought out for a minimal amount and I was the sole owner, but we had lost valuable time and my attention that the business needed.

All in all, he was a partner I never needed. I had been happy to wrap up financing for the new company but did not realize the high price and unstable partner I had in return. The under-explored option of mezzanine or private equity financing would have come at a higher price but would have been far cheaper in the long run.

Over the years, I have had several businesses with partners. Partners can be multipliers, deadly, or occasionally neutral. I was lucky to have escaped "deadly," but my experience is that partners should be a last resort. Many of us take care to set up the appropriate legal structure and documents to govern how a business with partners will operate, but no one can stop an irrational partner from filing a civil lawsuit and wasting time and money without cause. Since that ordeal, I have made efforts to buy out partners and wind down businesses where partners exist. I'm happy to report that this has been successful and highly gratifying.

We all likely spend time assembling the right management team, developing great products, and honing our customer service, but I doubt that many of us have spent as much time, or enough time, considering the importance of finding the best financing alternatives, let alone partners. You can always fire an employee that isn't performing. You can scrap a new product or redesign your existing line. You can revamp customer service and install a customer-centric service culture. But it's much harder to get rid of a partner.

While this partner caused a bump in the road, I learned a lot about not becoming overly confident and avoiding pitfalls later. In this case, it was being more self-aware, particularly with something as major as financing my new company without carefully considering how, or with whom, I would do this. My overconfidence, or hubris, made my aim off-balance when focusing on the bullseye of starting my business. Looking back, I can see that it was only a blip on the screen, but it did take me away from my business for a fair amount of my precious time. While I thought I learned that lesson well, apparently I needed to repeat that lesson one more time to make it stick in my mind.

The Friend

It happened as I considered the old saying "If you do what you love, you will never work a day in your life." Most people nod their heads in agreement at how true this is. Okay, I believe it too, but frankly I don't think it happens to more than a tiny fraction of people who work. I would prefer to think of being lucky as having a job that is challenging, rewarding, and not overly stressful. I would also add working with friendly and smart people. Beyond that, most of it is just a nice saying.

The same holds true for leading and managing a business. I don't love concrete and I don't love running a concrete business, but I am lucky to have all the other attributes described above. It has also provided me with a stable income and a good return on my investment, including my time.

At one time or another, many of us have thought about doing something we love. Maybe it's running a golf course, a horse farm, or whatever your passion may be. This urge can become stronger when you have some success and, maybe along with it, some capital to invest. It can also come along with a false sense of your own abilities and not recognizing your limitations.

I always thought I was smart and worked hard and the result was a successful and profitable business. The confidence that came with it was justified, just not universally applicable. I am good at running a concrete business, but that doesn't mean I am going to be good at running *any* business. It may seem obvious, but all too often we let our confidence turn to hubris and pay the price for it. As far as business goes, I've learned the hard way to stay in my own lane.

After exceeding expectations in the first few years of owning my own business, I felt confident that we were on a trajectory that would always be upward, and I had some time to look for other places to bestow my golden touch. The opportunity came when a friend and business associate talked to me about an opportunity to buy a car dealership. I listened with a lot of interest because I had always been a "gearhead," which is code for loving cars.

I had an opportunity to buy a Cadillac dealership from the daughter of the founder—who had just passed away. It was well established and had been profitable for many years. A friend of mine had been promised by the recently deceased owner that he would have a chance to buy the dealership when he retired, and his daughter seemed likely to honor those wishes.

We went through months of looking at the dealership and its financials, talking to banks and lining up financing, and discussing what fun this would be. Who wouldn't want to drive a different new car every month? After the contracts were drawn up and most of the negotiating was done, we began to see a shift from the daughter. Within weeks, she had changed her mind and decided she would keep the dealership after all. We weren't going to buy it from her—*but* we had been bit by the car dealership bug.

Over the next year, we explored other chances to buy a dealership and finally came upon a Dodge dealership for sale in Cincinnati. It seemed like a great location and we both liked Dodge trucks. They also had the Viper—a super cool V-12 sports car that looked and sounded awesome. We went through the same due diligence process and were satisfied, although this dealership had not been consistently profitable. The current owner confessed it had been a struggle and he was not able to turn it into the kind of financial performer he would have liked.

He was always honest with me but a good salesman as well. His explanation for its spotty performance: He was good at imports and not domestics. I knew this was true. He owned the only two Lexus dealerships in town, as well as the largest Honda and Toyota dealerships. He knew the car dealership business and was successful at it. He was convincing when he said that maybe this dealership needed someone like me rather than his large import dealership group. You could say he sold me on this logic but obviously I was the one buying it. I knew it was a red flag but convinced myself we could turn it around.

The first few months were a blast. I went to "car school" in Detroit to learn about being a dealer and spent about 50 percent of my time at the dealership. I felt engaged and was learning every aspect of the business. Our sales picked up some and it seemed we were on the right path. We were also sprucing up the building and spending money a little quicker than it was coming in. This seemed all right at the time, but the death spiral was beginning.

In the early 2000s, when we owned the dealership, Dodge had a good reputation for building pickup trucks and minivans but not much else. The market area was also saturated with Dodge dealers, with the same number of stores for past sales volumes that had shrunk by over half when we took over.

I also learned that almost every stereotype about car dealership employees was true. While this is not universal today, it still exists and existed in large numbers then. The foundational issue is that virtually every employee is paid a large percentage of their pay in different kinds of incentive plans. Salesmen are paid straight commission, mechanics a form of commission called flat rates, and managers a combination of small salary and commission based on their area of responsibility. It's supposed to be set up to reward high performers, but it ends up sacrificing quality, customer satisfaction, and can lead to unethical behavior.

So, we had a mediocre product in a saturated market with a less-than-honest workforce. After driving my tenth monthly brand-new car in a row, I realized we were not sustainable. Our unprofitable months were equaling our profitable months. This was on top of my biggest realization: I was not paying attention to my core business, the cash cow, and I did not really have a handle on this new business.

In the end, I was working ninety hours a week, over 70 percent of which was at the dealership. My partner and I tried different plans to get the business back on track but most included spending more money on advertising. None of it worked; it simply dug the hole deeper. We ended up selling the business and owing the bank money afterwards. It was a terrible experience or, at best, a very expensive education.

The car dealership violated almost everything I knew about business and how to hit bullseyes. I didn't understand the industry in general or my own company. I failed to hire good people. There was no culture inserted into the dealership, only the lousy, pre-existing one carried over from the previous owner. Worst of all, I failed to realize any of this and instead convinced myself that I could overcome what would be insurmountable obstacles.

While I have tried other ventures unrelated to my core business since then, they have all been small in scale with a limited downside. I learned my limitations as an investor and as a business manager. I also learned not confuse what I know with what I love.

If I had used my own knowledge and experience, I would have known this was a poor choice of a bullseye. It was small and fraught with environmental influences I could not control. Most importantly, neither I nor my team possessed the skills to undertake this venture. The possibility of acquiring those skills or personnel was essentially impossible, at least in the relevant timeframe.

An interesting postscript is worthy of mention.

As we were struggling with our Dodge dealership, but not ready to sell, my partner was approached by the owner of a Harley-Davidson dealership who wanted to sell. We both owned and loved Harleys so, as you might expect, we met with him and looked over his store. It was a great facility; customer traffic seemed healthy. He painted a rosy picture, and everything seemed positive. I gave him a list of information requests and we left.

Later that week, I received the information packet, which was fairly complete. Financial analysis was not my partner's forte, so it was left to me to slice and dice what we got. While the sales numbers matched what we were told, the costs were a bit high. In particular, the fixed costs seemed burdensome. The breakeven point would be a big hurdle every month. I also saw some debt that stood out on his balance sheet. I sent off a list of follow-up questions and information requests to investigate further. Meanwhile, my partner was visiting his store daily and falling in love.

When the additional information arrived, it explained their situation in more detail and made my apprehension rise. I was still somewhat interested, but even then, I began to worry about a new dealership combined with our current underperforming one. How would we swing it? Also, the debt went unexplained to the detail level I requested. I phoned the owner and probed further.

What I learned was curious, to say the least. The owner explained that he had a partner who was "not really a partner" but owned the real estate and was "owed some money." The debt I was concerned about was a note, but he seemed reluctant to supply a copy. He finally agreed and when I saw it, I knew I was out of the deal.

The note's onerous terms made it virtually impossible to get released as it had become past due. It also had provisions to repossess the real estate and/or take over the dealership. I alerted my partner to this and advised him that I was not at all interested. My normal bullseye analysis had returned. I was not going to let "love" get the better of me again.

Despite my admonitions, my partner proceeded and eventually bought the Harley dealership. Later, I learned that he spent months and many dollars trying to resolve the note held by the previous owner's partner/not a partner. It ended up costing my partner dearly in terms of his other businesses and personal savings. Unfortunately, it was never fully resolved at the time of his premature death a few years later.

I had dodged a bullet but was sorry I couldn't stop my friend and partner from doing the same. He had good intentions but let his heart get in the way. I took some solace in that I learned what I could and, more importantly, could *not* do. I would never attempt another venture where I was so unprepared to hit the bullseye. I would also not let a friend, even a good friend, talk me into being a partner in something that neither of us had any business being in.

Family

Family members are among the most common partners in small and medium businesses. Often, this is derived from ownership passing down through multiple generations. In this case, it is an unintentional partner of sorts. However, although many businesses are started with family partnerships, my advice is the same as with any other partner. Don't do it unless there are compelling reasons. What can start out as something that looks like a good idea and involves a family member can turn on its head just as quickly as any other partnership.

My father had always been my idol. I was the middle child of five kids with two older brothers and two younger sisters. I was the one who always wanted to hang out with my dad. I'd cut the yard with my plastic mower when he cut it with our Toro. I'd ride with him to work on Saturdays just for the fun of it. When my parents divorced, I always wanted to spend summers with him and often went to work with him.

When I got older, I would work at his company when I could, doing menial work or whatever he had in mind. In college, I decided I would work in the same industry as he was in. I liked it and liked being like him (that's three "likes," if you're counting). I didn't work for him though. He had a rule that none of his children would work for him in the business as an adult. I wasn't sure I understood that, but it was his rule.

This didn't stop me from going into the same type of business. I worked my way through the company in that college job and then started my own company, just like his. During this time, I'd still take trips to spend time with him at his company. I'd help analyze different things and give him advice that he asked about. It was that time in life when the son surpasses the father in knowledge although I'm not sure he saw it that way. However, it was clear that he was asking for more guidance and consultation about his business and rarely seemed interested in mine.

When I acquired a business in Indianapolis, I took on two minority partners. One partner was a large customer and offered the synergy of going into a new market together at the same time. The plan was that he would give us all his work in Indianapolis. The other partner was my father. I didn't need his money and, in fact, he invested no capital and only signed a loan as co-guarantor. Nor did I need his expertise or contacts. I did it because I wanted to be in business with my dad and hang out. Not good.

The business did well for several years and then hit the recession. It struggled but never failed to pay its bills or the loan payments. For several years, I had my other company loan it money to make sure it paid its bills on time. During these difficult times, our bank, as it did every year, requested financial statements and tax returns from the company and its guarantors. It was required in the bank documents we all signed. The other partner and I always sent these promptly. My dad complained about it, and then one year, at the height of the recession, flatly refused the bank's requests.

This started an ugly period where the bank continued to ask for and then demand the information. He would refuse and both would call me to complain. Finally, the bank had enough and called the loan. If we didn't pay it all within ten days, they would foreclose on the Indy business, padlocking the place and putting us out of business (not to mention wrecking my reputation, not my partners').

I don't know what changed in my dad. He was never out a dime and would not have been except for this. My main business was very successful, the Indy business was recovering and, in any case, supported by my capital alone. We ended up paying off the loan and soon after I bought him out.

I'm sure I'll never understand his reasons for sabotaging

this business. I've stopped trying to figure it out. As painful as it is to tell this story, it is worth it if it communicates the perils of partners, even if they are close relatives like a father. It underscores my belief that partners are best left to bridge players and golfers. Don't let sentimentality deprive good business decisions and pursuit of the bullseye.

Good Partners?

So, what are the circumstances that *would* lead to a successful partnership? Here are three requirements:

First, a good partnership would be defined as one where both parties are well aligned in the vision, strategies, and governance of the new company. The alignment should be tight, with clear and concise agreement on where the company is headed, how to get there, and who oversees what.

Second, a good partner should bring something you don't have and cannot acquire. It might be money but a better choice would be skills, experience, knowledge, or contacts that you don't have and can't acquire, hire, or find. This would also mean that the partners together have some sort of synergy. It means together they are more than just their additive merit and derive greater value together.

Third, there must be equal balance between the partners. This means that neither partner is overweight in more categories than the other. Partners should balance each other with roughly equal number of strengths and weaknesses but not in the same categories. They should complement each other.

Last Thought on Partners

The first section of this chapter was about a minority partner. He owned a small percentage of my company and I owned the majority. Our operating agreement gave me broad latitude to decide how the business operated and the extent of my authority. Despite this, he caused problems and disrupted the business for years. Don't be misled into believing you can totally limit your exposure to a bad partner by keeping their ownership low or by writing perfect legal governance documents. You can still suffer the consequences of partnership gone awry.

CHAPTER 4

TARGETING A CORE SET OF LOYAL CUSTOMERS

When I was writing the business plan, prior to starting my own business, I had fifteen years of experience in the same industry and in the same market. I had confidence in what we could achieve and set about writing the sales and marketing sections. We would target a core set of customers to develop long-term loyalty, and then supplement these with a smaller percentage of competitive-bid work. There were pros and cons to both types of business and a combination was the best approach for risk and return. That was our bullseye.

First Contact

Soon after we started the business in Spring of 2000, I got a call from Will, the general manager of a large commercial contractor. He congratulated me on starting my own business and asked how it was going. After we had chatted for a few minutes, he asked if I would come to his office the next day to meet with him and talk further. I eagerly agreed and we set a time.

I arrived at this office the next day ten minutes early. (Years earlier, I had developed a saying for my salespeople, "If you aren't ten minutes early then you are late!") I sat in the car and went over my pitch, which consisted of why I started my own company, where our plants were located, their production capacities, et cetera. I was hopeful that we could get the opportunity to do some of their work but there were challenges. This company did mostly competitive-bid work, which meant I had to bid every job, and they were known to be somewhat high maintenance. This combination can be risky. Bid work generally has lower profits and lower margins for error. On the bright side, they offered an avenue to substantial sales volume that could start quickly.

I went in and was led up to his office. To my surprise, it was not only Will sitting at this desk, but also three other people waiting for me. I sat in the only available seat, a couch that was lower than all the other chairs. (Nice try guys, I'd seen this amateur move before.) The conversation quickly turned to business. They wanted to know our capabilities and whether we were fully up and running at all three plants. I assured them we could handle whatever they had in mind and were prepared to go.

They went to some length to explain they were looking to establish a new supplier relationship with someone they could trust. They complimented me on the times I dealt with them with my previous employer, who was one of their current suppliers. We chatted some more, and they asked for my salesman to start calling on them regularly; they would send requests for bids on future projects. Will even mentioned that they would find a project for us to get started with them right away. The meeting had been a huge success.

The intermediate bullseye for the competitive-bid portion of our sales plan could be filled by more than half with a customer like this. The goal would be to bid competitively and slowly increase our share of their work. Some of this would have to be done by good old-fashioned quality and service. We had to exceed their expectations and certainly what was thought of as the current norm in the market. I got back to the office and shared the news. Then we began setting up strategy for this customer and building our business with them.

Over the next several years, we became their supplier of choice. This was the ultimate place to be with a competitive-bid customer. We sought and earned the right to have a "last look" on most jobs. This meant if we were not low on bid day, then we would have the opportunity to match the lowest price they received and still be awarded the project. This took extra effort and dedicated manpower, but the sales volume was terrific. They would quickly become our largest customer, amounting to 15-25 percent of total annual sales. Throughout this time, I would spend a fair amount of my own time servicing the account. That meant a lot of phone calls, lunches, meetings, and entertaining, but it was worth it at the time. It also meant some hidden costs that became apparent later.

Large customers and projects can be intoxicating. Volume can overcome many other problems, but it can also mask structural issues within your business. No one is immune to the lure of more sales and top-line growth, but businesses need discipline to understand if the relationship is sustainable and, more critically, worth the risks. Loss of a major customer can hit a business like the biggest recession you could imagine. Like a recession, that type of sales loss is usually not predictable. However, detrimental reliance on a major customer is often preventable.

Several years into this relationship, I noticed a trend in our internal data as this contractor became our largest customer. Although they already had our lowest prices, and therefore lowest margins, they had begun to demand even lower prices and were also becoming even higher maintenance.

"Higher maintenance" deserves some definition here. For us, it means the unexpected additional costs of servicing a customer or project. Specifically, this may mean 1) requests for costly product design changes without paying for them, 2) requiring more assistance/manpower on their projects, 3) modification or cancellation of orders without adequate notice, 4) attempts to deflect project problems onto us and other suppliers, and 5) slower payment of their invoices. If you know a customer with some of these traits, you can reflect it in their pricing. However, when a current customer begins to embody one or more of these traits, and they had not done so before, then they become maintenance issues or, more succinctly, profitability issues. This can creep up on you.

Beware of Change

This customer had begun to show signs of becoming a consistently high maintenance account. What used to be a give-and-take relationship had devolved into a full-on charitable account. At almost every turn, their problems were assigned to us. I would get calls for help, even if it wasn't our issue. It was supposed to be part of a long-term team effort, but it was getting further and further away from that. It was even laughable when their CEO asked my opinion on what his company could do to be seen in the best light by suppliers like me. I gave him some examples. Eventually, he asked me to write a list and describe my thoughts. I did so but chuckled to myself as I did it. I knew he had no clue; his company would not adopt a single suggestion.

This came to a head in 2010. We had been awarded a good-sized project and were looking forward to starting it in the spring. Almost immediately, their relationship with the construction manager and the owner of the project went sour. They were constantly disagreeing about some issue or other, and what the contract said. Soon, they dragged us into it. Their modus operandi was to pass the buck to their subcontractors and suppliers and not support us in meetings, even when they knew they were wrong. Academics call this deflection. We called it "run and hide."

About halfway through the project, we had a plant issue that caused a delay on one of the floors they were placing. They mishandled the delay on their end. It turned into such a disaster that the floor had to be torn out and replaced. Years before, this would have been handled differently.

First, they should have been able to handle the delay

and save the floor from being torn out. The expertise and manpower they once had on projects could have handled this situation without extra cost and certainly without a complete replacement. Second, they would have had a better relationship with their customer and be able to convince them that the floor was satisfactory to leave in. They used to spend time developing mutually beneficial customer relationships. Now, most of these relationships would turn adversarial once a project began. Third, they would have accepted at least part of the blame. Instead, they turned tail and ran. They refused to accept any responsibility and went even further by throwing us completely under the bus in front of their customer and the owner. (I think they even stopped and backed the bus over us for good measure.)

As we began to discuss who was responsible and for how much, their position grew more adamant. They were willing to arbitrate the matter but not to discuss it. They said that an arbitrator would help settle things "reasonably" and that we would all be satisfied it was fair. Later, I learned they were already losing money on the project and Will was under pressure to stop the bleeding. I knew we would be the blood donor when we scheduled arbitration. They brought in an expert who just happened to be the forensic structural engineer who led the investigation of the 9/11 World Trade Center towers failure. There was no reasonable discussion amongst business allies to resolve an issue—only a full-frontal attack.

The arbitration and subsequent settlement had more than their share of sordid details. I felt betrayed but also dismayed that I had not acted earlier on the accumulating data. It clearly showed that this customer was becoming less profitable and riskier. I should have been proactive, reducing our dependence on their work and beginning to limit the risks they posed. The former would have been straightforward and quick. The latter would have taken some time and effort but would still be achievable.

After the settlement, they made some efforts to make us feel valuable and always said they wanted our relationship to return to the "good old days." I knew those days were gone before this disaster struck and wasn't keen on trying to rebuild anything with them. We had already begun to transition away from their work and were succeeding in replacing their volume. By the third year, we had replaced all their volume with much higher-margin customers (price and productivity) and significantly less risk.

Two of postscripts to this story are worth mentioning. First, while we knew we were "firing" this customer, we never let on that this was the case. In fact, I would never fire a customer openly unless it was over uncollectable debt, dishonesty, or legal issues. We simply started pricing their bids higher to account for their lower productivity and anticipated maintenance costs and stopped matching prices if our initial bid wasn't low. I wasn't mad at them as much as disappointed at myself. We stopped repeating past errors and would only do work with them where we could attain a premium margin to account for the way they operate.

The second postscript is really for my sake. A small silver lining. As part of the settlement, we agreed to sign a note to pay about half of the settlement amount—about a quarter of a million dollars—as a credit towards future work, at a rate of $2 per unit purchased. The note was written with no end date and no interest charged, and they had no recourse if we never sold them anything again. I've never understood why they agreed to that, but they did. So, as mentioned in the first postscript, we began to price their work accordingly *and* we added another $2 per unit on top of that. It took over five years, but the note was paid off without costing us a dime!

Opportunity Knocks—Answer it!

Interestingly, we confronted a similar circumstance just a few years later. Our Indianapolis operations had struggled for several years and we were not successful turning it around. While we could sell more product if we chose to price our product lower, the margins were below my threshold for a reasonable return. So, we slugged it out for several years and waited for the market to improve. We soon had an opportunity knocking on our door.

Total Concrete Solutions, one of the largest purchasers of concrete in the Indianapolis market, had long been our customer but a rather small one. They accounted for less than 10 percent of our sales in Indianapolis. We were even smaller to them. I learned that our sales to them represented only 2 to 3 percent of their purchases.

That market had always worked the same way when it came to pricing such customers like this. Early each year, suppliers would send a new quotation with prices that would be effective April 1st and good for twelve months. Some customers would negotiate from that point, but most would simply make purchasing decisions for the rest of the year based on the quotations. We had sent them our quotation for the year and waited to hear back. They responded that the quotation was fine, and we should receive about the same amount of orders from them as the previous twelve months.

This lasted for a few months and then our salesman in Indy got a call asking for a meeting. When he met with them, they talked about a possible opportunity to get more orders and asked him to set up another meeting with his supervisor. He reported this to my sales manager, and I agreed that both of them should meet with them and see where it went. It sounded great but at the same time seemed a little odd. Total Concrete Solutions had always taken our prices and never negotiated. They just made purchasing decisions based on the new prices each year.

Our team met the next week with Total and got a little more insight. Each year, they spent a lot time analyzing suppliers and rated them on a variety of areas including service, quality, invoice accuracy, and, of course, pricing. Further, they said we ranked among the very best in every category but price and asked us to take a look at our pricing so they could consider giving us greater sales volume.

I thought it was an interesting conversation. Of course, I thought it was a great news and seemed like a big opportunity. I probed my sales manager more about why the change of course for Total now, after more than two months of new pricing, and despite the fact that they had never allowed re-pricing once a quote was submitted, and never done a mid-year change in purchasing patterns before. He wasn't sure but I could tell he was very excited. I decided I should meet with them and see if there was more to it.

My first meeting with Todd, vice president and a member of the family that owned Total, went well. I think we hit it off and immediately liked and respected each other. Alone, he explained the motivation behind all this. Their largest supplier, representing about 65 percent of their purchases, had met with them in early June and gave them an unexpected new price list. It was a substantial increase over the pricing level they had just received in April and was effective immediately. While Total felt they could pursue legal action, they knew it would be a long, drawn-out affair and not likely to yield a net positive outcome. So, they begrudgingly accepted the new prices and started planning a new purchasing strategy. Hence, the call to us.

I could tell that Todd was upset with his old favorite and dominant supplier but anxious to do what he could for his company. This meant finding new suppliers or existing ones that could handle larger volumes. I wanted to help fill this void very much. It was the answer to our lagging sales and a way out of a difficult time for us.

Over the next several months, we met regularly, fine-tuning our newfound relationship and ramping up business between our companies. We even agreed to re-open a plant that we had mothballed during the recession to supply a greater part of their needs. Their business with us increased about six times by the end of the year and Indy was again, after a long dry spell, profitable.

The following year, Todd and I kept up our regular communications with lunches, emails, and phone calls. They continued to increase their orders, and now accounted for about 50 percent of our Indianapolis sales, essentially maxing out our capacity. They now began to talk with us about investing in more production capacity. Everything was going very well, so I began analyzing our business model and what it would take to supply more of their needs.

We had hit our bullseye with this customer. It was an extreme success. We didn't have much time to celebrate or rest on our laurels, however, as Todd then presented us with a new bullseye. This one would take some careful consideration of how far we had come but also where it would lead next.

I take a little pride in being able to say I learn from past mistakes. From an academic standpoint, most people would challenge a business model that included 50 percent of sales to any one customer. (Most of us would challenge a model with that number at 40 percent, 30 percent, or even 20 percent.) There are other, unique factors to consider in every case, but the risk associated with such reliance on a single large customer warrants careful analysis.

Many of us make the basic mistake of convincing ourselves that taking on such a customer makes sense, and that the risk of a single, large customer will work itself out down the road or, worse yet, not matter. I would not state unequivocally that this is always the path, but I would say confidently that the decision deserves one's utmost attention and analysis. The hardest decision may be to say "no," or to alter the "yes" to acceptable risk parameters.

I never expressly told Todd "no" to making capital investments to increase capacity but told him we would continue to consider it. This was an honest answer. I decided my comfort level with an additional investment would rise if we were able to continue to grow other parts of the business and therefore lower, or at least balance, our reliance on their purchases.

Beware of Change—Part 2

A few years later, after continuing success with Total, the time came for new pricing for the next year. We submitted our prices and did not hear much from them for a few weeks. After a while,

I got a call from Todd who said our price increases were much higher than the other suppliers and it would be difficult for them to give us the same volume as in previous few years. Even though they were known to never allow it, I asked if we could re-submit new pricing and see if we could be more competitive. He reluctantly agreed.

We ended up submitting new pricing twice and were told we were still too high. Gone were the conversations about how great we were and that they wanted to develop a relationship with us. And gone were 90 percent of our sales to them. This happened almost immediately and without real notice. Yes, we were going to get less of their volume, but a 90 percent cut is horrendous. No amount of conversation helped. We were just out. Interestingly, the same supplier that had treated them so unfairly and so unethically by raising their prices mid-year, the same supplier who had lost a tremendous amount of Total's work to us, was now back to doing a large volume of their work.

Like many small and medium business owners, I was guilty of failing to appropriately evaluate opportunities for the long-term health of a business, particularly in relation to risk. To not completely consider the risk in undertaking a new strategy to hit your bullseye can be not only a tremendous disservice to your business, it can be downright deadly.

However, if we had decided to make the additional capital investments that they requested, and believed that is was somehow in exchange for greater sales volume that we could count on, we would have been left in the same position as we were originally but with greater investment in an unproductive market. Specifically, we would have borrowed money for the capacity and then left with greater debt to service with the same pre-Total sales. A real disaster.

There's a reason why independent accountants report concentration of sales among customers in financial reviews and audits. It's the same reason why bankers read those reports. It is a serious risk that needs to be weighed as part of a business's ability to be a going concern. Don't try so hard to hit your bullseye only to break your bow and arrow.

Keep an Open Mind

One last story along these lines illustrates how adjusting and being creative with big opportunities can pay off without taking on more risk. It is about being focused on hitting a bullseye and continuing to adjust your aim until the conditions are right to release.

One of our large customers, JRJ, was also a significant raw material supplier to us. We both sold each other material. The one who sold who more varied from year to year. The owners of JRJ are smart, fair, and honest, and their whole company generally acted the same way. Because we were a respected customer, I think they favored using us as a supplier.

Several years ago, JRJ was bidding on a Kentucky Department of Transportation project—one that was just outside our service area. We had considered bidding the project to customers like JRJ, but in the end, it was just too far a distance. We let the project bid without submitting a price to anyone.

It turned out that JRJ was the low bidder and would be awarded the project. They were happy about it, but I learned they were also concerned about the supply of concrete because it would need to be manufactured by a certain type of plant. While two of my competitors had this type of plant, JRJ was not thrilled about using either of them. The project's schedule was tight with liquidated damages for completion beyond a certain date. They needed performance from a supplier they could count on.

JRJ's president called and we were chatting about a number of things when he mentioned the project. He asked why we didn't bid it to him. I told him our reasoning, but he pursued it further. Eventually, he asked me to consider giving them a proposal, even though it was a competitive-bid project and they had already turned in their bid. I said we would look at it.

The only way we could give him a proposal would be to locate a mobile plant on the project site. This was possible as we owned several of these and one was idle. The difficult thing was they wanted it manufactured with a piece of equipment added to our plant that we did not own. This specialized piece of equipment would have to be ordered and would cost a significant amount—about the same as the plant itself. The size of the project was large but not large enough to pay for it. In looking to the future, I could envision using it on other projects, but it wasn't a sure thing. It could just as easily sit idle for years and was not a particularly good candidate for resale.

Rather than telling him that we could not figure out how to give a proposal based on his requirements, I met with the president and talked it through. He elaborated on their schedule and needs and how important this project was to him. Getting the project delivered to the Commonwealth of Kentucky on time and in specification would make a huge impression, and probably affect future work in that area. I could tell he was excited about the opportunity but also looking to find all possible ways to ensure his company would meet or exceed expectations.

As I sat and listened, I thought we could find a way to make it work for both of us. I took him through what we would need to do to supply him on this project. There were a few things beyond our control, such as the actual site and utilities that we would need their help with. He agreed that JRJ could take care of those and asked, "What else?" This was the turning point. I told him about the equipment we would need and that purchasing this equipment did not make sense for my company and there was no way to recoup the investment by ourselves. I suggested that if JRJ was to purchase the equipment and allow us to use it for no charge, then we could make it work. My reasoning to him included that he could sell it later or keep it and he would have it as an asset for future similar projects. It could be a competitive edge. He would have this equipment to allow me to use to bid to him but not to competitors unless he agreed and was able to rent it to me for an acceptable price.

After discussing it with his family and other managers at the company, he agreed to my plan. Over the next nine months, our two companies worked seamlessly together to execute the plan and hit the bullseye dead center. The representatives from Kentucky had even commented this was the best project they had seen in decades. There is no question JRJ performed well but we received a lot of credit for our part. Most importantly, we had realized an outsized profit on a project that was not possible without inventive thinking.

I believe a common mistake many small- to medium-sized companies make is to pursue unattainable or unsustainable bullseyes.

However, this doesn't mean that we ever gave up without exploring every possible way to take advantage of an opportunity right in front of us. No one likes to pass on big opportunities, especially game-changing ones, but innovative approaches to bullseyes can take different forms. This was an example of not modifying our own disciplined approach to what risks we take on to hit a bullseye, but rather modifying how we could do it.

This approach had the additional benefit of showing JRJ our willingness and determination to help them. It earned us credibility and future opportunities that our competitors would have a hard time replicating if even given the chance. Just as we benefited from a major customer, we also benefited internally as this added to our culture and strong bias towards customer service.

These three stories show remarkable differences in how customers can and do affect your business. The first was a customer we had but didn't want, the second was a customer we had but couldn't keep, and the third was a project we didn't think we wanted but got anyway. All worked out on our terms even if not quite to the best outcome. Keeping vigil over your processes and analyses is crucial. It will keep undue risks from threatening your business. However, the vigil doesn't have to stand in the way of new and extraordinary opportunities. Bullseyes aren't always directly in front of you.

CHAPTER 5

THE TRUE VALUE OF SUPPLIER RELATIONSHIPS

I think of suppliers in in terms of several different buckets. Being in a manufacturing industry may make my examples differ from service, retail, and other businesses, but they are still applicable across a wide range of experiences. My key supplier buckets are raw materials (used to make my product), fixed assets (trucks, plants, equipment), and regular replacement/maintenance (parts and services for fixed assets). All of these are strategically important as they have the potential to affect profitability. (For the sake of this discussion, I am disregarding commodity products such as office supplies.)

We spend about half our total costs of sales on raw materials. These are materials used for making concrete—like ingredients for baking a cake. And just as ingredients can affect the quality of a cake, raw materials can affect the quality of concrete. Although adjustments can be made to the concrete recipe, based on the materials used, there is still a tremendous impact on the finished product due to the quality and characteristics of the raw materials.

Due to this influence on the finished product, raw material suppliers can have a wide variety of effects on your business and your ability to hit the bullseye. They are as important as customers but in obviously different ways. Think of you and a key supplier as the two opposite ends of a balance beam. Ideally, the beam is level and equally weighted. Too much weight can cause the beam to become unbalanced and will affect the other side. As for a supplier, too much or too little weight may take the form of a quality issue, service problems, or even pricing problems from too much reliance or influence.

Suppliers Are Not the Enemy

Many businesses think of their suppliers as adversaries. Too often, interactions with suppliers are considered win/lose—or at least who can get the most out of the other. Typically, businesses want to negotiate the best prices and terms foremost, and of course, the best quality helps too. Mostly though, it is just the best prices. Since negotiating price is generic, many feel justified in telling some white lies along the way in order to get the best deal. Maybe they inflate the volume of business they will do for better pricing. Or, they may say, or at least imply, that they have a better price from another competing supplier.

This may seem like the normal course of business, and it may be so for many but in the long run, there are consequences to be paid for such behavior. It's easiest to explain this by recalling when a customer treats you this way. It can be hard to tell when they are lying or even just leading you astray. There are also the dreaded acts of omission. "Yes, I really do have a price that is 10 percent lower than yours," one might say, without mentioning that the price is for apples not oranges or they have not factored in other terms such as a payment discount.

Since raw material providers were my most important suppliers, let's look at a few examples of how they can affect a business.

I remember my first real job. I started at the company while in college and stayed for fifteen years, eventually becoming vice president and general manager. The owner was the stereotype for thinking of suppliers as adversaries. He felt justified in misleading them, often with outright lies. His justification often took the form of an allegation of wrongdoing on their part years before: "I am just getting back what they stole over the last ten years." Other times, he would just comment that this was the way the game is played: "Other people do it to us; why wouldn't we do it to them?"

As I was promoted, and as my responsibilities grew in the company, I had more and more occasions to be with him in meetings where this occurred. It made me uncomfortable at first and then downright embarrassed. Toward the end of my time there, it had become a major reason why I wanted to leave. I could no longer feel tainted by what I considered unethical and dishonest dealings. I remained vigilant in guarding my personal reputation by declining these meetings as much as possible and always being honest in one-on-one conversations with suppliers. This was a narrow line between being honorable myself and being loyal to my company. Above all, I never wanted to regret my own behavior.

At one point, a major supplier mis-invoiced a large order from us. It resulted in them undercharging us by almost $100,000. I saw the mistake and mentioned it to the owner almost in passing, intending to notify the supplier of the mistake. He took my passing comment and exploded with laughter. "Finally!" he said. "I'm going to get back at the bastards!" He made it clear that we would not notify them and keep the ill-gotten gains.

I tried to put it out of mind and convince myself that it wasn't my decision. However, it continued to nag at me and moved me closer to leaving the company. I knew it wasn't right. And I thought it would eventually come home to roost: Karma, cosmic justice, God, or something.

Almost nine months later, as the calendar year ended, we got a call from the supplier. They had found their error and asked, nicely, if we would check our books and verify that the mistake had been made and we owed them $100,000.

I took this to the owner and told him the news. Now, he exploded with anger. He went on about how we weren't going to pay it because it was too late and other such twisted logic. I let him get it out of his system and then stated the obvious. We would have to pay it. Despite knowing it himself, he still proceeded to call the supplier the next day and question the mistake, and when that failed, attempted to get a discount from what was owed. Eventually, we did pay the entire amount but our relationship with that supplier was colored by this episode from that day on.

After I left the company, I learned what had seemed obvious. This was a pattern of behavior that the supplier had detected, and this event itself caused a shift in how they treated my now previous employer. My only saving grace was that I had distanced myself enough from the owner during these meetings and conversations that it did not affect my own reputation. It was bruised a bit, but still intact.

Integrity Rules

The real value of my avoiding the taint of the owner's actions was apparent when I started my own company. By then, the supplier mentioned above was one of the largest in the nation for that material and I was starting my company from scratch with no customers. I went to many of the same suppliers as my previous employer used and asked them to do business with my new company. Three of the largest raw material suppliers nationally, including the one above, told me the same story. My former boss had threatened them and said he would never do business with them again if they sold me one ounce of raw materials. Apparently, these conversations were quite pointed and laced with profanity.

To my surprise, every one of them agreed to do business with me. Two of them, in their own way, told me stories of their dealings with my previous boss and how they admired my integrity and trusted me, despite not having any trust or respect for the owner. Despite my unease with being present when some of these incidents occurred, I had earned their respect and my opportunity to do business with them.

I'll never forget how important those relationships were and how they grew even stronger over the years. It also dramatically emphasized the importance of relationships with suppliers and led our whole company to embrace a philosophy of treating suppliers like customers. It is not a literal concept but a parallel one that is just as valuable.

I also remembered to reward such behavior in suppliers. Not all are deserving of customer-like treatment, but important and strategic suppliers can affect your bottom-line just as much as a big customer does. A great example came just a year into starting my own company.

Admixtures are the chemicals used to create certain characteristics in concrete that are needed or desired in different circumstances. Sometimes this may be weather-related or necessary because of construction methods or schedules. When I started my company, I called several different admixture companies and asked for proposals. I took these and created a spreadsheet and compared prices based on estimated purchase volumes. Two companies were very close in total cost so I asked to meet with each to discuss their proposals.

The admixture business is largely a commodity business and competitors knew each other's offering well. Both salesmen were knowledgeable and did an excellent job of explaining their company, products, and pricing. There were a couple of differences in what they proposed, so I probed them for more information.

One of the differences was in the quoting of accelerators—the chemicals that accelerate the hardening of concrete in cold weather and at other times when rapid strength gain is needed. The first company had quoted an accelerator that seemed to meet all the requirements we would need. The second company did not quote this type of product. I thought it may be an omission and asked about it.

I had known their salesman, Jeff Young, for some time and always thought well of him. My question was direct. The other company had quoted a specific type of accelerator and told me all their customers use it. I knew Jeff's company offered this type of accelerator (I had seen it in their catalog) and asked if he forgot to quote it. His response was remarkable.

He said, "Jim, I can quote you that product and it will do everything the other guy's will do. I'm sure my price will be competitive, and we'd love to sell it to you because we make a lot of money on it. But I gotta tell you something. The large concrete companies in the big metropolitan areas have figured out they can buy a cheap generic chemical and combine it with one you already use every day. Together, the price is less than half what I or anyone would charge for the product we have, and the performance is identical."

I stared at him. I could not recall having a conversation like this with a supplier. My silence led to one more surprise. Jeff told me his company would install the necessary dispensing equipment for handling the generic chemical in addition to his other chemicals if we'd like. I came out of my stupor and thanked him for the explanation and told him we would be in touch.

I learned later that the other supplier knew of the generic substitution but said nothing. I also later asked Jeff about our meeting. I asked why he volunteered the information when the only outcome was that I would purchase less total material from him. (I knew he was partly commission-based.) He matter-of-factly told me that he knew I would eventually learn of the generic alternative and switch to it. He didn't want me to hold the omission against him and, most importantly, he knew that his success was tied to my success, and he wanted to do everything possible to help me succeed.

Jeff landed my business that day and kept it every day afterwards. His honesty showed me that Jeff knew his bullseye too.

Obviously, not all suppliers are like Jeff or his company. Some are like my old boss, but most likely, the majority are somewhere in the middle. They are good most of the time, great occasionally, and unfortunately, not good at times. Over the entire time I owned my own business, my largest supplier was one of those in the middle, albeit usually on the good-to-great side.

When I worked for my former boss, I had the good fortune to establish a close relationship with Dave Lower, vice president of a major raw material supplier. This grew out of mutual respect and, to some degree, his distaste for my former boss and how he was treated by him. When I started my own company, he agreed to sell me material and, in fact, help in any way he could. This was a very big deal. This particular material was the most expensive component in my products; its price and performance had huge implications for my overall business. Also, that part of the raw materials industry was controlled and dominated by a few, very large companies. It was easy to get shut out of supply when there were periodic shortages or just priced uncompetitively.

For the first few years, we used Dave's company exclusively for two good reasons. We were too small to split our business with two suppliers for this material, and we strived for consistency in our products across all our plants.

Sidebar: The latter reason came from our belief that

consistency was as important as any individual characteristic in our products. (It was like McDonald's hamburgers. A Quarter-Pounder tastes the same all across the U.S. Maybe it's not your favorite hamburger but it is predictable.) Our industry could produce this kind of consistency regionally. It had not yet been done in our region, so I was determined to make it part of our differentiation strategy.

After those first few years, we had grown enough to support two suppliers of this material but our experience with Dave and his company had been very good. I considered splitting our purchases as other suppliers called on us but, in the end, Dave's company had service and quality that was above average, and I felt their pricing was competitive. Also, they vowed that if there was better pricing in the market, then they would always match it or make it right (credit our account) for any past months of overpaying. I was comfortable with this arrangement.

There were a few times over the next ten-plus years that they had to make price adjustments based on the arrangement. This occurred because the market was controlled by those few, very large companies. It meant that not every supplier sold to every manufacturer, so they tended to choose their customers and not pursue others. This is not atypical of an oligopoly, but it posed a risk for companies like mine. I had a great supplier, but they sold very little to the largest company manufacturer in the market. The risk was that they might not always know the lowest market price and inadvertently overcharge me. In turn, my bids against a competitor might put me at a disadvantage and either cost me profit margin or even the sale. I found out the hard way how this could occur.

About twelve years into my business, Dave's company

sold some assets in one of our markets to another supplier. We began doing business with this new supplier and came to find out that they charged significantly less in that market. We received an immediate price reduction. While I was happy with the savings, I was very unhappy with having been at a competitive disadvantage for so long in this market. By then, Dave had retired so I contacted his boss and asked to meet.

I explained the situation to him and got the usual list of reasons. He said we were charged the lowest price they charged anyone in the market. I noted the difference between that and the lowest price in the market. He seemed earnest in his offer to make it right and said he could credit the difference to our account for the last year. As the conversation wore on, I grew more and more frustrated. They had cost us margin because of their uncompetitive pricing. I could calculate that. They had also cost us sales where we lost a competitive bid. I couldn't calculate that, and had nowhere to even start. He began to see my point but still pushed back. I continued to make sure he knew what this might mean. A lost *marginal* sale cost more than any price adjustment could make up for. After some fairly tense final comments, we parted, and he agreed to call the following week with a new proposal.

That next week we spoke several times and I continued to push. My argument was that if I were to continue to be a 100 percent loyal customer that it ought to come with benefits. They should value my consistent and predictable purchases more than a company that splits their business. We finally came to the agreement to go back four years for price adjustments and to install a new payment discount of approximately 4 percent. This was to reflect the value of loyalty.

Overall, this was a huge win going forward but only a satisfactory outcome looking back. I had no doubt that the original arrangement had outgrown itself. I had failed to safeguard our company in the process. I did trust them but probably should have remembered Ronald Reagan's "Trust but verify" adage. This could have been achieved by parceling out some purchases to other suppliers to verify market prices while not jeopardizing the relationship with my existing supplier.

This all fits into the categorical risk of complacency. I was confident using this supplier to assist me in hitting my bullseye but was not diligent enough to realize the environment changed as the years passed. It was subtle. Maybe I started missing the bullseye but still hit the general target. It wasn't until I totally missed the target and shot the arrow into the woods that it became a problem. I blamed them for not doing due diligence in the market—to keep me competitive—but blame myself for not verifying.

Our philosophy regarding suppliers and the value of our relationships with them often drove our own company's actions. We wove our customer service standards into supplier standards and vice versa. Although there were often occasions when these efforts did not pay off or did not seem to have made an overall difference, they were beneficial. In any case, efforts and outcomes that failed to pay off did not deter us or how we conducted business.

Karma Rules, Too

 A few years into the start of my own business, we made the decision to expand into a new market. It required an investment to set up a new plant and hire the necessary people to operate it. At my previous company, we had operated in this market and I was knowledgeable of the customer base, so I developed a plan to market to a targeted group.

One of these targets was a company led by a father and son, the second and third generation of owners. The founder had passed on several years before and was somewhat legendary. The smart, hardworking father (and now current president) was a character too. He expected and got a lot out of his people. I admired how he was able to succeed through sheer determination.

I got to know the father and son when I was at my former employment. My boss and I would often meet with both father and son for lunches and to play golf a few times a year. The son was my age and we hit it off immediately. I remember him saying that he was glad he got to know someone his own age with so much in common in our industry. Occasionally, he and I would meet outside work and with our wives as well. I didn't think of him as a great friend and not sure I would have hung out with him without the work connection, but it was usually fun, and he was a customer. I continued to try and develop the relationship with the son, since he would apparently take over the business soon, and we were then only getting about 25 percent of his business.

About the time I left my employer and started my own business, I continued to stay in touch with the son. Conversations were always pleasant with him complimenting me and wishing me well. We also continued to see each other outside work some and it was always friendly. While I wasn't selling him anything during that time, he treated me as a friend and maybe more so, discussing personal issues and the like. Interestingly though, he was one of those friends that talk about themselves 90 percent of the time and rarely ask about you. While I think we tend to hang on to such "friends" too long, he was customer, in the past and potentially in the future.

Fast forward to when we were putting up the new plant. I again contacted the son to see if he would do business with my new company. I didn't think it would be terribly difficult to get at least some sales from him, given our friendship. His answer wasn't quite what I had hoped for. He explained he was already splitting his work among three other companies and that it would be difficult to fit me in. He said he would try and send us some orders but couldn't guarantee anything.

Several months passed and we had received only a few very small orders. I called again and he was nice enough, but it was an odd conversation. He dismissed the idea that the few small orders weren't much. As usual, he turned the conversation to himself, telling me about his personal life. As I was rolling my eyes on the other end of the phone, he started into a story that caught my attention. He had joined a new country club where my old boss (now a competitor of mine) was a member. He saw him frequently and felt bad about not buying from him. He said he needed to change that if he was going to be seeing him at the club regularly.

I was disappointed that I was not going to get any significant amount of sales from him, but astounded that he felt he could, or should, tell *me* a story about his newfound country club angst about my old boss and competitor. Really? I finally figured out that my time was best spent elsewhere. I wish had figured it out much sooner but I don't mind the effort. You must shoot the arrow if you want any chance at the bullseye.

A postscript to this story is especially revealing, going back to the supplier side of the equation. The son called a few years later and asked if he could park some of his equipment at our new plant site. This was the site for which I asked for purchases from his firm, although nothing of any consequence occurred. Because it was much closer to his work than his own equipment yard, he said it would save his crews time each day. It was just a favor with no offer of compensation. I was a tenant of the property which did not have any extra space. I could have just told him that and let him talk to my landlord about available land next to mine. However, I thought I knew the answer to his question.

The landlord, Larry Cornett, was in the trucking and transportation business. The son and his father before him had used Larry's company for most of their trucking needs, but that decades-long relationship had ended suddenly and completely stopped using him with no explanation or reason.

So, I said to the son, "Larry Cornett owns the property I'm on and the land around it. Do you know him?" He said he did. "Do you do business with Larry?" I knew the answer; he said he did not. I suggested he could call Larry but that he ought to do business with him before asking for a favor. He seemed surprised, so I took him through it. "Why would he do you a favor when you don't do any business with him? His dad did business with your dad, and you continued that but then abruptly stopped? And now you do business with his competitors but not him? How would you answer your question if you were Larry?"

There are undoubtedly things I don't know about the son and his business. I am sure he had reasons for his business decisions but maybe they weren't the best reasons. In any case, they were not communicated, except for the country club story. I do know that these lessons reinforce why suppliers should be treated at least fairly and honestly, if not as well as customers. These are strategic considerations, valuable both currently and in the future.

Suppliers are analogous to the equipment it takes to shoot an arrow at your bullseye. We'd all like to have the very best bow and arrows but sometimes the price may deter us. On the other hand, the cheapest bow and arrow may simply not be enough to hit the bullseye we seek. In most cases, it will be a balancing act. We determine some minimum standards, combined with our capabilities, and make the best possible decisions under the circumstances.

Therefore, supplier relationships are critical. To remain competitive, price is important but may be meaningless without consistent quality and responsive service. My company strove to be recognized as the leader in quality and service. It wasn't lip service. We wanted to occupy that part of the market where it was possible to earn higher margins and unique opportunities. To achieve our goals, it was crucial that our supplier *partners* were valued—and that they knew it. We always tried to demonstrate that regularly. Our ability to consistently hit bullseyes was as dependent on them as it was on our own performance.

CHAPTER 6

MARKET OPPORTUNITIES AND CHALLENGES

In many industries, sales are attained through a competitive bid process. The lowest bid matching the requirements of the buyer wins and gets to supply the business. At the other end of the spectrum, sales are acquired through presentations and proposals that match unique needs to goods and/or services offered by the responder. There is a vast middle ground where both processes are employed, and where the winner is a combination of price and offering. This is referred to as a value proposition.

While we would all like to get sales orders based on our unique offering, the truth is that price always matters. We all compete on price at some level in the process. In a perfect world, you would be able to see your competition's offering and completely understand its fit for the customer. This would include price. Outside of retail, this information is hard to get and comes with the risk that you may not have all the information you need. It also may be true that the purchaser, your potential customer, may not tell the truth or at least not all of it.

As an example, you may receive documentation, often called a Request for Proposal or RFP. This details what the buyer wants. It may include quantities, specifications, delivery, and other requirements. Your team analyzes this information and puts together a proposal. It may even be as simple as a quotation for a common good or service, such as five reams of paper or monthly landscape maintenance. When this is a routine part of your business, you often ask the buyer to give you feedback after the proposals are due. How was our proposal? Was our pricing competitive? Were we low?

When it is not purely routine, there may be opportunities to distinguish yourself from the competition. You may point out exceptions to an RFP that you wish to take, or make suggestions where more value can be derived from doing business with you. This is the value proposition part (sometimes also called "value engineering") where a proposal contains a response and some options that are outside the original RFP scope of work. These are the opportunities to win the bid and prove that you can offer more than your competitors.

Often, these are conversations that take the form of bid reviews, scope reviews, and other dialogue that seeks to clarify a bid. It is where marketing and communication skills come in handy. It is part of selling yourself to the purchaser, but it is also the chance to shine and where new relationships are born.

Perhaps most importantly, this phase of potentially winning new business—where you can acquire market information and intelligence—can have the largest impact on the goal of maximizing profits. Sometimes, such information may be publicly available, but in my business and many others, it comes primarily from communications with potential buyers.

Learning from the Wrong Approach

My former boss used to set product pricing himself. It was one of the last responsibilities he hung onto and had not passed to me. His method was to shoot from the hip, with no tracking of previous projects or prices and margins, jobs we won or lost, or historical data with specific customers. He relied on his memory and how he felt that day.

As our daily, weekly, and monthly sales volume would vary, always trending up and then down and then back up again in a cyclical fashion, his attitude toward bidding and pricing would change. Sometimes sales volumes were slow for a few weeks and our bidding would reflect that with lower prices. Other times we would be very busy, and the impact was opposite.

Legally, talking to your competitors about such issues would be a violation of anti-trust laws. So, to remain out of prison, he would constantly guess where our competitors might price a project and then set our pricing accordingly. In a longer view of things, we might have tried to get our prices up and therefore improve our margins. Without breaking the law, it takes work to understand your competitor's behavior and adjust your own. Unfortunately, actual costs, overhead, and desired profit margins were not part of his thinking.

My boss liked to think he influenced the market more than he did. We were comparable in size to our competitors, and no one had enough mass to move the market on their own. So, it was a challenge to develop strategy that would maintain or grow sales *and* maintain or grow margins. Before bids were turned in on large projects, I recall he often would tell me he was going to "send a message," either to the market in general or directed at a specific competitor. It seemed he was often going to pay retribution to them for some past transgression.

Although I watched many of these "messages" go out, it was not surprising that the intended recipients never received them. It was as if our "Enigma" machine didn't work. Message in and nothing out. The same was true if we were the intended recipient. We'd never even guess there was some message in a competitor's bid on a project—only that we didn't get a job and they were the reason for it.

There were two problems with all this. One was never understanding that the market wasn't receiving our so-called messages. I never saw or heard anything to indicate that they did. In fact, the feedback was usually that we were very low in our pricing or that our competitors were upset that we were getting all the work (although always at ridiculously low prices). The second problem is that we weren't listening. My boss wasn't paying attention to signals that the market was giving.

Arrogance, cockiness, hubris, and lack of humility are good descriptors of the root cause of this issue. My former boss was myopic in his pursuit of sales over a balanced approach of sales increase and margin improvement. His real blindness was not being receptive to market information, and never in a timely manner. He and I were usually aligned on the target we sought but diverged on how to get there. We almost always had all the resources necessary to hit the bullseye. The big difference is that one of us received information about the environment and the other resisted it.

Whether you are the largest or smallest in a market, pricing trends can be finicky and at times illogical. That means they must be monitored constantly and diligently. Only by doing this will a business be able to operate strategically and begin to maximize profits.

Obtain and Analyze

When I started my own company, I was adamant that we would be the "experts" at the environmental factors regarding sales. If we were to hit our bullseye, we needed up-to-date and accurate information. Merely intuitive forecasting would not do. We began by creating a matrix of information for every project we bid on after it was awarded. Only after years of collecting this data were we able to identify trendlines and develop useful forecasting tools.

The Indianapolis company we acquired was a bit of a mess when we bought it. To a large degree, this was one of the attractions. It offered good assets in strategic locations but was not a well-run company. The upside potential seemed big.

Once we took over, we analyzed their customers and looked back over five years of data. The data lacked the color and depth to make it valuable beyond just the raw numbers, so at first we had to make some assumptions in order to maximize our sales effort for revenue and return.

This initial analysis showed two things. It identified a handful of customers that cost way above average to service their accounts. It also showed us several products that had way below average margins. We adjusted our bid process to address both issues, raising prices on all products to certain customers and raising prices on a few products to all customers. We knew this would cost us sales as we adjusted our bidding but also were confident that we would shore up our overall margins.

Our plan worked well. In the first few years, we grew revenue, thanks in part to a good economy but mostly by jettisoning low-margin sales and replacing them with higher margins. It wasn't rocket science but solid analysis and determined execution. I felt our regular analysis of the data and continued fine-tuning would serve us well into the future. So, I handed over most of this continuing work to my sales manager, who demonstrated a grasp of this feedback loop system of analysis and adjustment. My oversight of the bid process was reduced, since I thought the tools I put into practice were well-understood and would guide our bidding.

Several years after our entry into this market, sales were leveling out and we were entering into the recession, although we didn't know it at the time. We just knew sales were slowing and there was added pressure to maintain both revenue and margins. Our sales analysis work continued as before, and I was now reviewing the sales manager's work each quarter. It seemed competent and we had added some qualitative information to improve it further. This included pricing patterns that emerged from customers, types of work, and geographic locations. Some of these trends would even get down to a useful "micro" level.

However, sales continued to fall, and we recognized that

a recession had arrived. We scrambled to maintain sales and largely to avoid "losers," or sales of some products for the sake of volume. One of our saving niches was the infrastructure work still being done, some of it from federal stimulus funding. We had developed a solid following of customers in this market segment. One particular product was continuing to be a top seller and we held on to those sales. Its margins were about average, but its volume was a saving grace. My quarterly review reinforced our strategy to protect this niche.

As the recession deepened, we maintained sales in this niche. I trusted my Sales Manager and his analysis seemed complete, even while we were feeling the brunt of competitors' attacks in every other sector. So, at one point during the very worst recessionary year, I began to have a series of meetings with our customer base. These were particularly valuable, helping me learn what I would not have any other way.

One such meeting was with a customer that always gave us some work but only about 5 percent of his total. As we talked, I probed him about what would change his mind to give us more work. His answer was simple. Our pricing was always on the high side except for one product. He said we would always get his work for that product, but we were 8 to 10 percent higher on all other products. He ended with, "I don't know how you guys do it, but you must have figured out how to make it cheaper than anyone else. You save me a bundle every year on that stuff." Inadvertently, he had given me a lot of information. It didn't matter so much to him because purchases of that product amounted to very little of his total purchases, but it mattered a lot to us. We sold a ton of it elsewhere in the market to other customers too.

I went back to the office and began to investigate our

bestselling product to see just how successful it was. As I dug deeper, what should have been a success story began to turn my stomach. I found we rarely lost a bid on this product, and when we did, it was because it was packaged with other products and only a small percentage of the total bid. This meant if it made up most or all of the bid, we won, and if it was a small part of the bid, we lost. Mostly, it meant we weren't as good as we had all convinced ourselves we were with this market niche. We were just low-priced. Later, with other confirming conversations, I learned we were extremely low-priced on this product.

Over the years, the market had moved on the pricing of this product and we had not noticed. Although our data gathering continued, it was not complete. We failed to detect an important and costly trend. Instead, we simply congratulated ourselves for being so successful in selling this product. Since it did not show itself as an outlier in margins versus the other products, we kept congratulating ourselves. We had been overly focused on catching the lowest margin sales and how to transition out of them that we failed to see the lost opportunity in our bestselling product.

We took time to verify our new findings and identify just how much margin we had been giving away. We wanted to maintain the sales but maximize the margin of those sales. It would take a phased-in strategy with almost constant checking for feedback so as not to overrun the market. We would raise prices slowly but methodically, hoping to eventually reach the point where we still might be lower than our competition but not much more than token amounts. We also wanted to stay vigilant in monitoring our competition for any changes in their pricing of this product.

This was an interesting if costly reminder to keep our eye on the bullseyes for all parts of our business. In the recession, we, like many, became laser-focused on cutting costs and eliminating low- or zero-margin business. We also tried like hell to get additional sales, but it became a fight just to keep the sales we had and break even. This drove a lot of energy and focus on costs but not the needed extra focus on the market and our bidding process. Unfortunately, we focused on "problem" areas and failed to look for opportunities in the bidding aspect of our business. We felt grateful for the niche sales and didn't bother giving it the same attention as lower performing products or customers. It wasn't a squeaky wheel but it sure needed oil.

In general, it was a reminder to not let circumstances overly dictate focus. In a recession, we should have kept focus on the best parts of our business just as much as the worst parts and looked for improvement in both. In good economic times, it might be the opposite that can misplace attention. This possibly would take the form of focusing our bidding process too tightly on growth areas while not fixing the less appealing bid areas.

Just because some arrows are sailing off into the woods, it doesn't mean you shouldn't give the same focus and attention to the arrows hitting the target but missing the bullseye. Both are indications that a change in aim is needed. Both are worthy of your attention.

The same can be said for negotiated projects as these are likely to involve bids where there is some complexity or new elements involved. This is an opportunity to successfully bid a project that requires more than just an analysis of the RFP and specifications. It can also be the opportunity to put all your market intelligence to work to meet the challenge.

Information Equals Opportunity

The largest project we ever bid on was a hydroelectric plant—an electric power generation plant, usually situated on a river, diverts the river into a turbine and then returns it back to the river. This project was on the Ohio River, conveniently only a few hours from our office. However, the combination of building a river diversion system and a power plant at the same time was so complex and demanding that almost all our regular competitors declined to bid.

This is the type of exciting project that my company thrived on. Our bid would require considering not only difficult product specifications but also demanding delivery requirements. Our excitement as a management team came from the challenges of facing anything difficult and demanding. My own excitement was even higher as projects like this offered the chance to compete with a smaller number of competitors. The significant additional risk, complexity, and demands of the project also meant the potential for much higher margins.

As the bid due day approached, I was busy fielding inquiries from companies that we would bid to as well as completing a final analysis of our bid. The combination of a privately owned hydroelectric plant and the U.S. Army Corps of Engineers' specifications for construction of anything on the Ohio River meant that everyone was confused about something on this project.

We had researched a similar project bid a year earlier. I had made several calls to suppliers and contractors to gather as much information as possible. Based on this investigation and the size and scale of this project, my company would have had to create an entire new division to service the job. Our annual capital expenditures for this project would exceed the rest of my company's expenditures by a factor of three.

Our bid went out and we waited for feedback. Since it was a private owner, there was no public opening of the bid, and we all had to wait on the owner to find out who would be awarded the project. As was typical for projects like this, the owner ended up negotiating with the two lowest bid contractors. As a supplier to the contractors, we would have to wait to hear from them as negotiations continued. Occasionally, we would get a call for a clarification or two, but for the most part, the phone didn't ring. Finally, the negotiations seem to be winding down and I felt a decision was imminent. This is mostly because at the end of negotiations on such large projects, it almost always comes down to money. As the two contending contractors began to make their final price cuts, we got calls to see if we could make some price cuts too.

This is where our effort to understand the bids of the previous, similar project paid off, as did our work to find out what other suppliers had bid to contractors that were no longer in the running. I had a good idea of where our numbers needed to be and was comfortable with them. There was only one wrinkle that had yet to come, but I was expecting it.

Terry, the vice president of one of the last two contractors, was somebody I trusted and had a good deal of experience dealing with. He was far from being a pushover, but I always knew where I stood with him and knew when he was pushing me to a limit. I didn't have to wait long for his call. When I answered the phone, Terry was his normal, cordial, but direct-to-the-point self. "We need to meet ASAP," he said. "My final numbers are due to the owner three days from now and I need to talk through your bid. I also have some ideas that could help both of us win the job." That last part ("some ideas" and "help both of us") made me a bit uncomfortable. I knew him well enough to know this wouldn't be a simple conversation.

The next morning, we met and went through our bid. Our supply of materials would form an unusually large part of his overall proposal to the owner, making our meeting of utmost importance to both of us. After reviewing our bid, Terry got to the point. He started out with "What if we look at this differently than normal projects? I don't think there is any way we get to the number I need without being creative." The word "creative" from him was usually code for costing me money.

Over the next several hours, Terry and I hammered out an unusual deal. We agreed to treat the supply as a quasi-joint venture where his company would shoulder all the downside risk and we would be guaranteed a minimum profit on our work. It would require an unusual amount of co-managing the project but we both felt our two companies were up to the task. The downside for me was that the minimum profit guarantee was at the low end of what we would expect to make. I made one final proposed change to the agreement. It was that our company would split excess profit over a mutually agreed budget. If we brought the project in under budget, we split the savings equally. We were done and shook hands.

While this type of arrangement in construction may have been done in the past, I had never heard of it nor even thought of it. It was unique and truly a win-win. Terry got his overall number down to where he expected he would be awarded the project (he was). I got relief from the risk of any adverse issues but kept a profit-sharing arrangement if things went well. None of this would have been something I typically would have agreed to, except for one fact. All our intelligence-gathering on this project pointed to the fact that the bid pricing that was needed to be awarded the project was below where I was willing to go.

Without our focus on gathering information about bidding this project, we would have stuck to the lowest bid acceptable to us and not been awarded the project. By understanding this dynamic, I knew our only chance was to work through an unusual arrangement with Terry to keep our foot in the door. We ended up with a smaller profit but with no risk and a potential to add to the profit. The smaller profit, especially on a project this size, was a hell of a lot better than being left on the outside looking in.

Looking Past the Obvious

Sometimes there are challenges that just don't seem worth considering for the sake of sales. We have had our share of unreasonable requests, specifications, or other demands that made us pass on some potential sales. Most of the time they were truly unreasonable—either impossible to perform or with too many risks. Other times, what seemed impossible or too risky to many of my competitors would become an attractive opportunity to us. It may be either a perception thing or maybe just out of one's comfort zone. In any case, some of these became opportunities for us to build a competitive edge because we were willing to understand the bullseye and develop all the resources to hit it.

I got a call one day from a customer for whom we had done quite a bit of work. They had been contacted about repaving Bristol Motor Speedway, one of the most iconic racetracks in the country. It was a unique opportunity for many reasons, offering construction challenges that permeated every aspect of the project. We agreed to look at bidding the project, but I was not confident that it was for us.

For starters, at just over a half mile, the track itself is short. This meant the banking turns were a severe thirty degrees. To give you an idea of what that looks like, imagine walking up the track at a turn, stopping, and leaning forward with your hand out. Just before you topple over, your hand will touch the wall above you as you lean on it. It's hard to believe that cars can stay up there and don't just fall down the track.

This banking meant we would have to develop a concrete that could be placed on these banked turns and stay there until it cured out and became hard. It also had to be *workable*, so the construction crews could get it into place, and *finishable*, so the surface could be smoothed properly for a high-speed race. This product development and design was especially challenging.

The other daunting aspect was that this repaving would have to be done between Bristol's two races each year—one in the spring and the other in the summer. They were only about three months apart. Normally, such a project might have a nine- to twelve-month schedule but this would be compressed into less than half of that. To meet this schedule, we would have to operate twenty-four hours a day for most of the time.

To top it off, this project was not very big—about the size of a typical, medium-sized commercial project. We would have to undertake all the complexities and schedule demands for not much sales volume. It was the reason so many others weren't interested in bidding the project, but it intrigued me, especially if we were able to plug in outsized profit margins.

We ended up winning this bid and doing the project for several reasons. We had the expertise to do the long and tricky work involved in developing the right product—including a full-size mock-up section of the banking turn. We were also willing to meet their schedule. For this, we would have to bring a full-size concrete plant to Bristol and set up in their parking lot. This would begin on the day after the first race. Finally, they accepted our pricing proposal for all of this, including a record unit profit for my company.

We committed to these rigorous requirements because we knew we could do it, albeit with a lot of committed resources. We also knew there would be limited competition which meant opportunity for outsized profit. In the end, our willingness and capability to hit their bullseye meant we could negotiate a lucrative contract rather than merely being the low bidder. Although the negotiations were not easy, we knew we had built confidence in the contractor and owner that we were the only logical choice.

Willing to Challenge Convention

There are occasions when an opportunity for sales appears reasonable, but the competition looks insurmountable. We have had times when we shied away from spending energy on a bid or proposal just because the competition is a goliath or had some other competitive advantage. We never had unlimited resources, so picking our fights with competitors always required a considered approach. Do we have a legitimate chance? Is the potential profit worth it? Will there be other ramifications?

Just such an opportunity knocked when the Indianapolis Colts were planning a new stadium in downtown Indianapolis. It was to be a downtown centerpiece, providing the opportunity to play games in freezing temperatures thanks to a retractable roof. Once again, product and construction schedule were going to be challenging.

> We were asked to bid the project at about the same time we were negotiating an acquisition in the region. Although the company we were acquiring had assets we could use for the project, their capacity was below what was required, and they did not have the management expertise to execute such a large-scale commercial project. In any case, since the acquisition was not complete when we bid on the stadium, we looked at it as a standalone project bid.
>
> Most importantly, we had to consider the competition. Unlike Bristol, this was in the middle of a major metropolitan market—one served by one of the largest, privately owned concrete companies in the country. They would no doubt be very tough to beat on price and service.
>
> Our ace in the hole was the fact that we had not closed on the acquisition of the other company. If we had, our focus would have been on upgrading their facilities and management to meet this challenge and then bid the project from their existing facilities. Instead, I looked at the project as a standalone, with the idea that we would put a concrete plant on-site. This sounds easy but putting a concrete plant in downtown Indy (or any major metropolitan area) when

we had never been there and did not have political ties or influence would be difficult at best.

We ended up working hard to convince the winning contractor and owner that we were worth the risk. This meant many hours of planning and presenting our proposal to engineers and project management leaders. It meant showcasing our experience and knowledge. It also meant negotiating with suppliers that did not typically work with the market-leading competitor to give us an advantage with the promise that our acquisition would lead to more work.

Our hours of effort paid off as we were able to negotiate every aspect, including the hard-to-find location next to the new stadium for our plant, at favorable prices and terms, and barely beat our competitor in the final bid negotiation. Ordinarily, we would not have spent the time pursuing a project when such an ominous competitor loomed large. Logic would indicate that we didn't have a chance. Then again, you hit exactly 0 percent of the bullseyes that you never shoot at.

A laser-like focus on understanding all the external factors influencing these projects gave us the opportunity to hit the bullseye. Under normal circumstances, we may have just called off the shot or made a shot destined to fail. Instead, we used information to reassess what the bullseye was and take dead aim at it. In the end, these were successful projects for us and significant feathers in our cap.

In all these cases, information was the indispensable tool. Without it, our aim and efforts would have taken place as if we were in a vacuum. Carefully gauging the environment, especially its changing nature, helped us escape losses and earn extra profits. My company also learned that there is a learning curve that steepens as the number of unknowns increases. In other words, as the number of unfamiliar elements affecting your aim increases, the greater the need for current and accurate information. I don't think this type of investment ever failed to pay off for us.

CHAPTER 7

SECURING THE RIGHT PROFESSIONAL SERVICES

Professional services are those services and advice that are required for the success of a business but that are not within current management expertise. Attorneys, accountants, and consultants are the most common examples. At times, their work or advice can be mundane or perfunctory. At other times, it may tip the scales and influence a specific course of action. In the end, it is always the business owner's responsibility to make final decisions or whether to engage others in these services.

In most small- to mid-sized businesses, the choice of a law firm can seem like a mundane decision. Assistance in business filings, standard contracts, or collections often do not often take more than just average legal competence. However, when the need arises for advice in a particularly strategic or sensitive area, you may need some critical expertise. Having the right attorney can be invaluable. Interestingly, the best time to find the right attorney is not always the same time as when the need arises.

Attorneys

I would always advocate for having an ongoing relationship with a high-quality attorney from the start. This might cost a little more for mundane matters but will pay off in preventing unwanted future consequences. It will also give you a trusted resource for issues you don't anticipate. It is not a good place to cut corners, just to save money, or put off until the last minute.

I once had the unfortunate experience of being sued by a partner—the one I described in a previous chapter under the subtitle "The Worst." The outcome was a major victory and seemed obvious to me. The one thing I could not figure out at the time was *why*. Why did he pursue this path? Why did he go to all the expense and time when the outcome could not have been seen likely to benefit him? My initial reaction was that there was some personal animosity, and that he was pursuing a sort of justice in his own mind. To a large degree, that may be true. However, as time has passed, I have come to believe he was misled by his attorney as to his chances in prevailing in the lawsuit. At the very least, there was an omission of the risks, costs, and likely outcome on the part of his attorney.

A quick review is in order. The partner had become adversarial and demanded unreasonable amounts of information that we did not have. I granted him access but did not generate information that we did not possess. We had data but did not process it into the kind of information he desired. I offered that he could do that on his own time or at his own expense, which resulted in a long two-year legal battle that ended midway through a trial with a settlement. The settlement left him without any ownership in our companies—all for a relatively small amount of cash that would not cover his legal fees or expert witness costs.

The point at which we settled was after his side had put on all their testimony and evidence and the judge had granted our motion to throw out most of his claims. It left our claims completely intact and him very vulnerable to owing me a large jury award.

After ruminating about this for months and maybe a year, talking to my attorneys and others, I concluded that his attorneys must have led him down this path. He was of average intelligence with a high school degree and worked for his father in a small family business. He also was not overly sophisticated in legal matters. My conclusion is based on his inability or unwillingness to look without bias at the case before him and consider the risks and rewards. It was as if he was willing to go through a long and costly legal fight without knowing where his bullseye lay or what might affect his ability to hit it.

His attorney was a well-regarded litigator in a large and prestigious firm. However, we were in the middle of the late 2000s recession, when there was not much legal work to be had. My own attorneys spoke of this during the trial and at other times before and after. They also commented that this had caused many attorneys to take on clients and matters they wouldn't have touched in normal times.

My partner's hubris and personal issues caused him to

initiate this matter, but his attorney cemented his fate by either encouraging or allowing him to believe he could win. Maybe an attorney is hired to advocate for his client, but I can't imagine an attorney of mine letting me proceed in such a matter without sternly laying out the facts and likelihood of success. And frankly, trying like hell to talk me out of it.

This led to terrible consequences for him. He lost an investment in two companies that would go on to become successful and eventually sell for a huge return. He paid attorney fees for two years and consulting fees for a high-profile expert witness to prepare a report, which was thrown out at trial along with his testimony. The small amount I paid in the settlement would not even begin to cover those expenses. The failure to find and hire an attorney that could appropriately advise and guide him through this process had cost him well beyond anything he could imagine. It is a regret he will have to live with, but one that could have been avoided.

Attorneys can be incredibly valuable counsel for many types of transactions and other strategic endeavors. However, they are also fallible, just like the rest of us. It is paramount to remain clear-minded and as detached as possible when hiring and using an attorney. The ultimate decision to use an attorney or, more importantly, to follow their advice is still incumbent on the business owner. Attorneys offer advice, which is just that—advice. In the end, it is only you who will have to live with your decisions.

I often liken attorneys to the way we look at our own doctors. Some of us might be very careful and go through some due diligence when it comes to selecting a doctor. Very often, we do not. We may go to a doctor because our parents, or a friend or spouse, did so. Maybe the doctor was simply close to our home or office. There is also a lot of momentum to continue using the same attorney, to continue pursuing the same course, even when the facts have changed. This inaction does not help our aim when trying to hit a bullseye. It is simply a double-down of the original bet and can detrimentally overlook new risks or threats.

I have been guilty of this. I have used my general counsel for matters outside his expertise—where he would recommend a partner. I remember two specific examples—collecting past due accounts and a construction arbitration matter that had outcomes that were not critical to the existence of my company. However, the lawyers involved would not have been my first choice and did not achieve the outcome I was looking for. In both cases, my own due diligence of interviewing the attorney and reviewing the case before it proceeded would have resulted seeking other counsel and, potentially, a better outcome.

To continue the doctor parallel for one other point may be informative. Later in my career, I have relied on an attorney for a second opinion. As with a doctor's second opinion, I asked a different law firm to review my situation and the applicable law and give me advice. This has happened both in the early stages of a matter and in the middle of a matter. In both cases, I was honest about what I was asking for and the circumstances, including that they were not primary counsel on the matter nor was I looking to change counsel. The advice I received helped me understand that there are multiple ways to look at a matter, such as varying perceptions or predictions of outcomes by different attorneys. In turn, this helped me in dealing with the primary attorney handling the matter.

In many ways, the most difficult assessment is with choosing the right attorney for the matter at hand. If you need to hire an attorney, it is probably because there is a question whether you can or should do something. It is rarely black and white and usually involves elements of judgment that make it crucial to have the right counsel. It is often also a matter of the relationship between client and attorney. An attorney can be like a client or have a completely different personality and skill set. It is up to you, the client, to determine what is best to hit your bullseye.

What's a Good Attorney? (Not to Be Confused With "What Good is an Attorney?")

I found my own attorney in an atypical way. He represented the opposing side in a real estate development transaction I was a part of. While my first dealings with him were not confrontational, I appreciated the way he handled the matter and represented his client. It convinced me to hire him for a similar matter a few months later, and then eventually he became my primary counsel on most matters. I valued, above all, his responsiveness, competence, honesty, and fairness.

Responsiveness meant that he responded appropriately. If the matter was urgent, he would call at night, on weekends, or while on vacation if it was warranted. He also was always timely with other attorneys. I rarely heard him accused of being tardy in his responses to the other side.

Competence meant that I never found that he wasn't prepared and knowledgeable for the given circumstance. It didn't mean he knew everything immediately, but it did mean that if the agenda for a meeting included a subject matter, then he was prepared to discuss that subject.

Honesty meant that he would tell me when I was wrong or taking too much risk. It also meant he would tell me when I would be better served by another attorney, based on the subject matter at hand, even if that included recommending me to another firm. He would also be honest regarding his partners and associates. He would freely tell me how different partners worked and whether he had any concerns with their ability to handle a matter. He also always mentioned their rates and efficiency, so I could gauge how expensive they may or may not be.

Fairness meant his fees were reasonable. I never felt he was padding my billings with associates' time or inter-office conferences. He wasn't cheap but I never questioned his time. I found that especially refreshing when recommending lower-cost associates or higher-priced partners, as the situation required. Once, when he recommended a very high-priced partner, I appreciated his saying, "She charges double what an associate would charge but she'll do the work in less than half the time."

Accountants

Accountants would seem to need much less thought and consideration in choosing. It appears much of what they do is black and white, or a matter of competence. I think this is a misconception and a little of "apples versus oranges," particularly as it relates to tax accountants.

When I started my business, I used one of the "Big Four" accounting firms.[2] I used this firm because my previous employer had used it, and I knew many of the partners at the local office. I don't remember thinking they were particularly innovative, just competent, and the Big Four name seemed to lend credibility to my new company.

I learned that my little start-up was not a particularly important client to the firm. They were certainly competent, as far as I could tell, but I never felt like I was getting any value added to the basic services of an annual audit and tax preparation. It seemed almost like a vending machine. We fed in information and they popped out a report and tax return. Thank you very much and see you next year.

For the first several years, this seemed fine, but I came to believe that my association with a Big Four firm wasn't really important to my banks or anyone else and that their fees may be higher than what we could get elsewhere. I decided to seek proposals from other firms to check this out. We contacted two regional firms and one local one. The regional firms had multiple offices and thirty to fifty accountants. They typically had several on staff that were experts in certain fields or concentrated in certain industries. The local firm had a single office and fewer than ten employees—essentially a grown-up mom-and-pop firm.

The local firm was a good fit for a business that needed an accounting department but couldn't afford one. They did the books for a lot of companies on a regular basis. I

---

2   The original term in the 1970s and 1980s was the "Big Eight," as there were eight dominant accounting firms. Over the years, mergers and a major scandal (Enron) reduced that number to four today.

didn't feel this was a good fit for us, as we were growing significantly by then. We ended up with one of the regional firms and were happy with their lower fees. They were very capable and serviced our account well for many years. I felt no reason to even seek proposals from other firms.

After our first decade in business, we spent considerable time looking at—and sometimes acting on—several acquisitions, mergers, and joint ventures. I often consulted with our accounting firm about different tax laws, deal structures, and other things that would have significant impact on whether to do a deal or not, and how to structure it. Unfortunately, I was often unimpressed. Their service lacked timeliness often and their answers were not clear. They were not dumb but just didn't put in the time to be right the first time I asked or deliver it when I asked. Two pretty big things.

Eventually I decided to once again put our accounting business out for proposals, this time trying a different technique. I asked most of the bankers and other business owners I knew who they used or respected. Then I researched them and settled on three finalists whom I contacted through a current client of theirs. I told each one that I was certain to move my business but wanted to meet with them, including whoever might be on the team that would service my account.

These conversations were interesting in three ways. First, I could see how each team member presented themselves. Second, I could see how they interacted amongst themselves. And third, I could see what questions they asked about me and my business. At the end of each meeting, I asked if they would review my last three years tax returns and give me an analysis of them and any suggestions. I always offered to pay them for this although no one ever took me up on that offer.

I ended up with a firm that hit on all cylinders during this process. In the meeting, I could tell each team member was confident and competent in their area. They exuded a "not my first rodeo" feeling that made me comfortable. They also interacted well. It felt as if they were friends by the way they conversed and held respect for each other, not merely colleagues at the office. I could sense a team spirit that I likened to my own company. Lastly, they found a decent savings in my returns (on self-employment taxes) that would have paid for half their fees each year.

I've stayed with them ever since. They continue to show they are engaged in my business and its issues and willing to dive in when asked. They are also proactive. It shows in our regular meeting when they ask me probing questions or multiple "what-ifs." It is a much better fit for my business and I believe has brought value in terms of actual dollars as well as assisting strategically.

Whether you receive professional services from a firm or person, they are supplying you with a valuable input for your business. Your success may very well depend on your choice of advisors. Due diligence and careful consideration are critical to choosing someone in a manner that includes evaluating many factors, including price. Of course, the balance of price and qualitative factors will change, based on the product or service supplied.

Besides the obvious, I would emphasize one important consideration. Take into account the potential long-term value and sustainability of the relationship. We would all rather spend our time on customers than on professional services. An advisor's real value includes reliability and trust that transcends today's delivery. Choose your critical professionals carefully based on a balance that leans toward how they can contribute to the long-term value of your company.

An ideal relationship with a professional service provider allows you to spend your valuable time focused on the strategic issues of your business. They should improve their offerings without request and help avoid problems you didn't identify. The ideal ones allow you to focus on the bullseye with minimum distractions and maximum assistance.

CHAPTER 8

IN SEARCH OF
GREAT PEOPLE

Almost all CEOs will say that people are their most important asset. It's not only true, but people, your employees, can make or break most companies. I would go further and say that a company's key management are the single greatest determinant of success. I've met a lot of outstanding employees in all sorts of businesses. Virtually without exception, they work with quality and high-performing managers and leaders. Those key managers are what drive execution and the ability to hit your bullseyes.

The Critical Hires

When I started my concrete company, I had recently resigned from an employer of fifteen years to start a direct competitor. Most of my former employer's management reported to me at the time I left, and I knew how valuable the key ones were. I planned to staff my new company with the best and knew that recruiting at least some of them was crucial to my success.

As I contemplated the most critical management aspects for my new company, I realized that operations management was a high priority. I could not cover all the operational needs without some help from several high-quality, seasoned managers. Financial management was not as critical because I could carve out some of my own time for CFO-type work. Sales would be a challenge, but my own efforts would also cover quite a bit of ground there. I just couldn't manage three plants, forty-five trucks, and all the employees needed to operate them without help. And it needed to be top-notch.

Luckily, I knew four top-notch operations managers who had worked for me at my former employer. Business can be brutal to survive, and I wasn't about to not pursue all four of them. My calculation was that I could start the business with one of them, although my preference was two. If I got all four, then I would slot them in other areas until we grew sufficiently. Frankly, it was also a strategy to deprive my former employer and future competitor of their talent as well. The icing on the cake was that these managers would also help recruit our plant operators, equipment operators, drivers, and others.

Just because these four managers liked and respected me did not mean they would come running with open arms. I had to make sure I sold them my vision of the new company, namely treating employees better, higher customer service standards, increased quality manufacturing capabilities, and more. All in all, the bullseye was to be the best in every way.

These were lofty goals and a hard-to-hit bullseye, but capital and a plan to achieve this was my focus—and it was coming together. I made the call to all four and invited them to my temporary office one night at 7 PM. After they all showed up, on time, and we shook hands and chatted, I led them into a conference room and laid out my plan.

I could tell they were interested, maybe even enthralled, at the prospect of joining my new company. I had prepared extensively and covered all details including a phantom stock plan that would give each of them a percentage of the appreciation of the new company. We spent over two hours going over the plan and answering questions. It went very well but I also knew that leaving their current employer would not be easy. One had been there thirty years and two had been there almost twenty years.

I spent the next week or so talking to each one sporadically. They all seemed to be leaning towards joining, but I was nervous. I knew better than to be too confident despite the initial positive feedback. I began to think about what I would do without at least one, and whether I could proceed or needed to pause and reconsider. Finally, as the commitment deadline approached, I started to hear back. My first choice by far, Lou, was in. Shortly afterwards, Jeff said he was in as well. He had the least experience but was smart and hardworking and would only improve over time.

The other two had a change in heart and reversed their initial decision to join. I was saddened about it but thrilled with the two that agreed to come aboard.

Some positions require the very best. Maybe it's because it is an area you are not knowledgeable or experienced in. Maybe it's capacity issue. In this case, it was an area I could not afford to fill with an average performer because of our bullseye of being the very best and my ability to step into that role was limited.

Lou and Jeff stayed with the company until the day I sold it. They both reaped the reward of ownership through the phantom stock arrangement. They blessed me every day with an effort that was second to none, treating my company like it was their own and putting herculean effort into it. Altogether, Lou and I worked together for thirty-two years. He was my indispensable man; I never doubted his judgment and effort, and I never worried about whether the shop was minded when I wasn't there.

Don't Stop Pursuing the Right People

Although I felt that operations were a higher priority than sales, the latter was constantly on my mind. I could do only so much on my own and needed to find the right salesperson. This would be uniquely critical as we would initially hire only one person. As we discussed this position, we knew the one person who was the right fit—a standout among the many salespeople at our former employer. It was not merely that he was selling the most; he was honest, knowledgeable, and hardworking.

Our prospect, Gary, had been in the industry for over thirty years but had the energy of a twenty-five year old. He had always impressed us. So all three of us made the pitch to him to come join our team. We knew he liked us and had respect for what we were doing. We knew he would always listen and consider what we had to say. However, in the end, he said that while he appreciated the offer to come aboard, he was going to be loyal to his employer and stay there until something changed.

We later learned that our former employer was also sweetening the pot for almost every other key person there. By then, we had hired over two dozen of their best, along with Lou and Jeff.

Over the years, we continued to call Gary to see if he was ready to change his mind. Lou did this regularly, in a non-obtrusive manner. After almost ten years, some things changed at our former employer; they hit a very rough patch. It was our opportunity to make a pitch that would finally succeed. Gary joined our team, albeit later than we wanted and made an instant impact. Just a few years later, I made him sales manager.

Gary was an immediate hit, not just with our customers, but also with fellow employees. Always a smile on his face and willing to do anything for a fellow worker. He was as good a team player as anyone we had.

Even though we didn't hit our bullseye with salesmen at the beginning, we never stopped pursuing it. We employed several salespeople before Gary came aboard. Some were good, some not so good, and some outright mistakes. Despite this, we maintained our bullseye and went about hitting it as best we could. Gary had a much-admired quality that kept him away from us for so long—loyalty. Despite being aboard a foundering ship, he stayed with our former employer until it was too obvious to ignore: being loyal there no longer held any value.

Challenging Times but Good Lessons

Most companies will never have to deal with unions. This may make this section of the book seem like one to skip, but I hope you continue to read on. I learned many lessons from my experience with unions that applied to other aspects of my business. Although it was an experience I would have rather skipped, or read about from someone else, it was invaluable.

Current statistics explain why most of you won't have to deal with unions. Today, only 10.7 percent of the workforce, or 14.8 million employees, is unionized. That is down significantly from 1983, when comparable statistics were first kept, and the rate of union employment was almost double. Currently, 34 percent of public sector employees are union. These are mostly teachers, police, and firefighters. The private sector has a unionization rate of about 7 percent. The highest rates are in industries like utilities and transportation and warehousing.

My experience was mostly with the Teamsters who represented concrete truck drivers. This was common in the Midwest many years ago. Back then, most metropolitan areas in my industry had union drivers while rural areas were a mixed bag. I remember stories told by my predecessors about union negotiations and strikes. The strike stories were the most entertaining. There were tales of guns, fights, and cars following management home at night. Hearing about Teamster chiefs who would drive black Cadillacs and intimidate anyone who dared cross a picket line was funny, scary, and seemed like something out of a movie. My indoctrination came very early.

At age twenty-one, I had just transferred to a new college near home. I got a job at a concrete company to pay for college in March of that year. I had worked for two weeks when the drivers decided to strike. In that time, I had met almost all the drivers and was friendly with them. They treated me as the nice but naive college kid that I was. Being the lowest man on the management totem pole—not really being management at all—I knew some about the circumstances of the negotiations and that a strike was possible. However, it just seemed outside of my reality, not a real concern.

Very early one morning, I got a call before I left for work. The drivers were striking and there was a picket line. I was told to be careful but come in. They also told me of a back entrance that I should use. It was 6 AM and raining—like a perfect setting for a movie. I drove to work anxious to see what awaited.

I went through the back entrance and parked my car. It was still dark, and the management had assembled in the big, ten-bay maintenance facility. The company president began telling us the plan: we were all to drive trucks that day, through the picket lines, back and forth all day. We would supply concrete to our customers just as if it was a regular day. We were told to be careful, take our time, and always lock the doors on our trucks. Just another day for a college kid at work before afternoon classes.

For the next three weeks, I drove every day. The strikers

were mostly nice to me. Some would even wave as I went through the picket lines. A few gave me their meanest looks or gave me the one finger salute, but I was generally given a pass. A few instances were more intense. On the third day, a few of the Teamsters followed me to a project site where I was to deliver concrete. I pulled on site and began to unload. Within minutes, workers from other areas of the project began to stop work and assemble nearby. They were members of other unions and were there to protest my presence. It was my first scare as the crowd swelled to over one hundred workers, all stopping work to protest my being there.

After what seemed like an eternity, the foreman came over and told me to stop. He said he was going to terminate the delivery and get me out of there. He was getting threats and couldn't afford to have so many workers standing idle on the timeclock. I wasted no time getting the hell out of there. There were some taunts and shouts as I left but I was glad to be leaving. As I drove back to the plant, I could only imagine what that could have turned into.

This was my first experience, making a lasting impression of the potential power of unions. Not only were they able to affect how we did business, but also, they could rally other unions to support them and make a big statement. At the time, I don't know that I was aware enough of the circumstances to appreciate their influence. However, I was aware enough to know I didn't like it.

The strike began because the company was seeking a wage reduction. It was 1985, and it had fallen on hard times. Its very existence depended on restructuring wages that had risen too fast over the past decade but now rendered it uncompetitive with other concrete companies.

The strike ended when drivers began to cross the picket line after three weeks had passed. One late afternoon, after management had been driving concrete trucks all day, they started coming into the office. First, an older, slightly built guy, Booker, came in and said he just couldn't pay his bills and wanted to come back to work. This could be dangerous, since his union cohorts might find out and punish him. It turned out that he was only the first. By the time we were ready to go home, a dozen or so drivers had come in. The strike would be over.

I don't think you could say either side won or lost. Both were in danger of going broke and both needed each other. It was a calculated risk for each that luckily ended well—or at least better than it could have. The alternate was for the company to go broke (which it would have if the strike lasted another few weeks) and many people would have become unemployed.

Weeks passed and I began to see a change. As the drivers resumed driving and managers resumed managing, the company began to rebound and discovered a new esprit de corps. Slowly, the employees began to "row" together, in the same direction, and we gained momentum and a firmer financial footing. I saw the lost alternative of *not* having to go through that strike to wind up where we did. It was a valuable lesson, but one that could have been learned in a more positive way. I began to see the strike as something that could have, and should have, been avoided. I was developing the foundation for my own philosophy of how to treat employees and how to run a company.

Two years later, I had begun to take on more responsibility in the company, and another Teamster union contract was about to expire. It became my job to negotiate the next contract with Merle, the business manager (essentially the local CEO) of the union. He and I had minor dealings in the past. He was nice enough but definitely old-school. In his late fifties, he had been a union member all his life. I called to discuss the new contract.

He and I met for breakfast—just us, no one else from his union or my company, including members he represented that were my employees. It was my first negotiation. I thought I was prepared; I had gathered a lot of information on wages and benefits and what my competitors were paying. I even had some statewide and national statistics. I was ready to share all this with him and lay out my logic when he got right to the point. "What can you give my guys?" he bellowed after taking a drag from his cigarette. (It was back when you could smoke in a restaurant.) I started to lay out my reasoning when he interrupted and said, "Just tell me what you got." I didn't know how to react, so I just pulled the bottom sheet of paper from my stack and handed it over.

He took it from me and stared at it for a minute. Then, he looked up and said, "Jimmy, it's not bad, and I knew something like this was coming since the strike two years ago. It's still a little light. I need another twenty cents on the wages and ten cents on the pension. You do that and we can finish our breakfast and talk about something more interesting." (As an aside, I hadn't gone by the name Jimmy since I was ten, but that never stopped Merle and other men his age from calling me that.)

I was astonished but did my best to keep a poker face. Of course, that first offer wasn't going to be our best offer, it was just a starting point for negotiating. What I really didn't expect was that his counter was almost exactly where I hoped to end up. Before I could answer, he pushed a bit more and said, "Come on, we got a deal? It won't kill you and you can sell this to your boss." He was right on both accounts. I agreed and we shook hands. Twenty minutes tops and breakfast hadn't even arrived yet.

We ate breakfast and talked football and politics. We laughed and shared stories—mostly his. I couldn't believe what had just transpired and mused about telling my boss what a shrewd negotiator I was. We finished breakfast and were about ready to leave when he put his hand on my forearm. He looked at me and said, "Jimmy, before we go, let's agree how this plays out. We've got the first official negotiating session with the drivers later this week. We're still going to do that. You start with this sheet." He patted his suit pocket where he had put the paper. "Then, I'll start in. I might call you a few names and your boss worse. I'll probably pound the table and get up and walk around. Then, I'm going to tell you what I've GOT to have for my boys. We can go back and forth some but don't get in a big hurry. We'll just put on a little show for my boys."

If I hadn't been surprised before, I was now. He was proposing to put on an elaborate play for his members—my drivers—with me as the co-star. I paused long enough for him to get up and flip the check to my side of the table. I didn't know what to say so I got up and grabbed the bill. Soon, I was following him to the checkout and quickly paid it. We walked outside and he just grinned. He stuck his hand out to shake and told me it was pleasure doing with business with me. Finally, I mustered some words, "So, we got a deal on my proposal, plus twenty and ten cents, right?" "Hell yeah," he said. "Just help me with my boys!" He laughed, and we shook hands again. Later that week, we put on the play he had written and had a new signed contract later that month.

This stands out as the most successful (and weirdest) union negotiating experience I ever had. We both won, but it didn't feel so good in front of the drivers when we met later that week. Even though I got what I wanted, it felt dishonest in front of the drivers. I didn't want to be part of that again, and I didn't want my relationship with any employees to be based on something that approached a sham.

This experience laid additional foundation to my thinking on employee relations. I regretted that I didn't have the direct and honest relationship with them that they expected and deserved. And I did not want to be painted with the same brush as Merle. Even with this win-win, it was not the type of win that I wanted or what the drivers deserved.

Six years later, I began what first appeared to be an awful episode with a union but which turned into a valuable, long-term experience. I had graduated from college with both a BS in Management and an MBA. I continued to be promoted and given more responsibility, so I decided to stay with the company. By then, I was made vice president and general manager of one of the largest concrete companies in Ohio and business was going very well. Based on research I had done, we decided to put up two new plants in Cincinnati. They would be brand new and would require all new employees.

> Putting up two greenfield plants within two years was a logistical challenge. The physical aspect of purchasing and installing the plants was well within our capabilities, but hiring employees was the real challenge. Qualified applicants were scarce, especially in the numbers we needed. We were attempting to hire fifty new employees, but because our employee turnover rate was 20 to 30 percent, the work of finding, onboarding, and retaining that many new positions

was even more difficult.

About the time the second plant was operational, we began to detect some union activity in the form of leaflets and informational material found around the plants. It would be left in the cabs of trucks or in break rooms. We also heard from a few of our loyal, anti-union employees that there was a "buzz" out there. People were talking about how they could get higher wages and better benefits with a union.

We did not dismiss the rumors and printed material we had found. We tried to gather and dispose of it as quickly as we found it and engaged in conversations with the drivers more often to see what more we could find out. After several weeks of this, we thought we were being effective in quashing the uprising, but we weren't. In retrospect, we moved too slowly and not aggressively enough to stop our drivers' interest in union representation. The union, a Teamster local, was already in our midst. They had convinced several drivers to support them who were, in turn, trying to convince others.

The union upped their campaign and became more overt in their actions. They would stand in front of our driveways to the plants and hand out flyers. They'd stop our trucks and talk to the drivers as they would come and go. Of course, we tried to stop this, but it was a tightrope to walk. You can tell drivers not to stop and threaten discipline if they do, but this plays into the union's hands. Management can suddenly be seen as heavy-handed, abusive, and adversarial.

After a few more weeks had passed, we received a letter from the National Labor Relations Board that we had been dreading. It informed us there was to be an election to see if the union would represent our drivers at the two plants. We knew this was the ultimate fight to keep a direct relationship with our drivers or let the union come between us.

We hired a consultant whose advice we trusted and followed their strategy throughout the campaign. It was a weeks-long, non-stop war of words. The union made ridiculous and blatantly false claims. We fought back and provided information of our own. We talked endlessly with the drivers, mostly one-on-one but also in small groups. We tried to count employee votes ahead of the election, using a list of our drivers and our best guess of how they would vote. As the election drew near, we felt we had a slight edge and hoped we would prevail.

Election day came, the votes were tallied, and our best guess of the outcome was not a good one. We lost by a small margin; the union would represent our drivers. In my autopsy of the situation, it became apparent that we did a lousy job on several fronts. Our recruiting and hiring process for drivers had not produced the type of employees we had elsewhere in the company. We had lowered our standards in order to get people hired. We hired hastily and did not onboard them as thoroughly as we usually did. To top it off, they were not located near our other employees who could have been an asset in the indoctrination process.

We licked our wounds but immediately decided we would pick the next fight. The vote margin was small enough that we felt we could have won with more time and an improved strategy. Federal law dictates that there couldn't be another election for at least a year, so we made it our goal to have another election in a year's time and to win it. Of course, this would be up to our drivers to decide, but ultimately up to us to achieve.

We missed our bullseye by a long shot. It was painful. We had felt prepared and capable of hitting our bullseye and yet made enough mistakes along the way that we missed. The only upside was that we learned a lot. We took this experience, and the hard-earned education it provided, and began to figure out how our next attempt would hit the bullseye.

Our strategy was simple this time. We would not use a consultant or inundate the drivers with information and meetings. We would operate our business as usual and treat our drivers the way we always had. It wasn't complicated. I made sure my managers did what they did best: treat everyone fairly, consistently, and humanely. We were fair with hours worked and opportunities for overtime and advancement. We were consistent with our pay structure and application of work guidelines. Finally, we treated everyone like peers and teammates. This last part was not just a show. It had to be done earnestly and the managers had to live it.

I was blessed with some very good managers who were relieved to be able to do their jobs the way they know how, rather than following a consultant's script. We started off slowly but began to get momentum with driver sentiment. Negotiations over a contract were not going well, but while the union blamed us for the lack of progress, we remained professional and polite with our drivers. They had to figure this out for themselves. We couldn't force it or speed things up.

Ten months went by and there was still no contract with the Teamsters. We did everything to the letter of the law in negotiating, but we were not going to agree to a contract that put us at a disadvantage with our competition or jeopardize our goal of another election. A quick contract agreement would have all but killed any plans for another election in the near future. The drivers would have simply forgotten that there were any issues or any reasons for an election if we signed a contract.

By the one-year anniversary of the election, we began hearing from more drivers that they wanted another election. Some of the stronger supporters of the union had left the company and others were having second thoughts. My managers made great use of the time. Every day, they proved to the drivers that we were a good company to work for and that the union was in the way. Within a month of that anniversary, we received another NLRB notice for another election.

We resisted the urge to hire a consultant for the final push to the second election. I did not want to vary our actions or appear to go into an unnatural mode of employee or business management. I told my managers to keep doing what they had been doing for the past year: treat everyone the same way and don't make any decisions based on the coming election. We were not going to change who we were.

As a management team, we could all sense the tide had turned. With each passing day, we were encouraged by our drivers' actions and words. We were back to doing the right things as managers and leaders of our employees, and they were rallying together. This time, though, the rallying was with us, not against us. The support was palpable.

Election day number two came. As with all NLRB elections, union management can be on the property to observe balloting. They usually show up in force at each location and serve as a reminder to vote for the union. For the first election, they had cajoled and acted like the drivers' best friends, which drove me crazy. However, the second election was a pleasant surprise. Not one union official showed up for the balloting at either location. Apparently, they had concluded they would lose the election and decided it was

> not worth their time (or didn't want to be present for a losing
> vote count). We won by a large margin. I knew we had taken
> dead aim and hit the bullseye.

In some areas of business, when I don't feel especially well-versed
or informed, I have relied on consultants for advice and even leadership on certain issues. This happened most often in legal and
tax accounting matters. Other times, it might be a permitting or
zoning issue or, in this case, a human resources issue. We had used
a labor attorney to make sure we were compliant with labor laws,
but we mistakenly also chose to use a consultant to help us try to
win the first election. While their advice was always educated and
coherent, it was never combined with what my managers and I
knew about our business and our employees.

I disregarded my own gut feelings and experience by hiring
an expert in unionization efforts. On the surface, it made perfect
sense. In reality, it took us out of our comfort zone and away
from practices that worked and were appreciated by our drivers.
I think the drivers even sensed our lack of authenticity during
that first election drive. It ultimately doomed the first election
but was very instructional for that following year. Both managers
and drivers came out better for the experience—more loyal and
dedicated to each other. It was a lesson learned the hard way but
appreciated by all.

When I started my own business, I was confident that I could
handle any unionization issues that came up, but I was also determined to avoid unions if possible. Even though I had decertified
four unions by then, I knew the time and effort was costly in terms
of dollars and in the toll on everyone involved. By starting from
scratch, with no employees, we had an advantage versus buying a

company already operating with employees. It gave us reason to be optimistic that we could assemble the right group of employees and create a sense of teamwork and togetherness from the start.

From the beginning, it worked well, and our quality of hires was significantly better than we had experienced at my former employer. There is something about the type of people who will apply to work at a brand-new company with no customers. They tend to be more outgoing, curious, hardworking, and willing to take on responsibility. They also became a team quickly. Everyone was new and on the same footing so there was no existing hierarchy or cliques. Although we made some mistakes in new hires, it was a very positive and rewarding process overall.

In the sixth year of my new company, things were continuing to go well. We had some of the most productive and positive employee attitudes that you could ask for. The investment in time and effort with our employees had paid off very well. We also had never received any indication that a union was attempting to influence our employees or that it would have succeeded if they did. I remained confident that my knowledge and experience would make unions a thing of the past for my new company. Unfortunately, I seem to learn the hard way how confidence can be misplaced.

> In that sixth year, we pursued an acquisition of an existing company in Indianapolis. They had four plants and were doing about a third of our business volume at the time. As we did our due diligence and checked out the fixed assets, we also spent time talking to management. They seemed to be competent but not overly impressive. This made the acquisition more attractive, as we felt our management could improve their operations and profitability.

We planned to close the deal towards the end of the busy season. While it was not imperative, we felt we needed to keep as many of the employees as possible to get off to a good start with their customers. We did not want any lag in production or service. I talked to the owner several times about their hourly employees and probed him for any issues. He assured me that there were no union issues and very few problem employees. The closing date was moved up, and I made the fateful decision not to interview the hourly employees individually but just hire all of them. I thought that when the busy season was over, during the inevitable winter layoffs that occur in our industry, we would just lay off the lowest performers and then not bring them back in the spring.

We closed and took over the first week of November. I drove to Indianapolis the night of the closing and held an employee meeting. I showed up at the hotel where we had arranged the meeting and greeted many of them gathered outside, smoking and talking. I walked in and they followed. They seemed a somewhat quiet bunch, which I chalked up to the normal anxiety over a new owner and employer. There were about fifty of them assembled in one the hotel conference rooms.

I had made notes on what I wanted to talk about and started in with my remarks. Everyone was glued to me as I talked. It seemed to be going well as far as I could tell. A lot of head-nodding and a few smiles. I was proud of my company and told them of how well we had done over the last six years. I knew the previous owner, who was a son of the founder, did not have his heart in the business. His father had died in a plane crash a year before and he just wanted out. I imagined most of the employees could sense this and would appreciate our taking over.

As I ended my remarks, I told them that many of their questions would be answered in the days and weeks to come, but that I'd be happy to answer any questions they had if I could. Someone in the front row raised his hand and asked, "Are we going to get a raise?" This was not totally unexpected, but it surprised me a little. Money first. I said we were still assessing the market and what was paid by other companies but that we would have an answer to his question soon. In the meantime, I added, everyone would still make the same wage rates they had made with the previous owner.

I thought it was a good answer and was in fact what we were going to do. He must have thought differently. He stared at me for a second and then turned and walked out. That was another surprise, but I had some momentum from the day including my remarks in the room, so I quickly asked for the next question. This went on for about a dozen more questions before we ended the session. I told them how I looked forward to tomorrow and the beginning of our future together. Everyone filed out; many said a few pleasantries or smiled and shook my hand. All in all, I thought it went as expected—except for the first guy. It bugged me and I would find out why soon enough.

A few months later, we received notice from the NLRB that our drivers wanted to vote on union representation. I felt blindsided. The former owner swore he knew nothing of the sort was going to happen. I believed him but later found out the unionization effort was months old when I showed up and they simply tabled the election effort until we bought the company. We had walked into this problem without a clue.

We lost the election quite handily. We used the same consultant as we used with my former employer, believing things would be different. They sent a different person to work with us, but the result was the same. This HR consulting company had an excellent record with union elections. I didn't blame them for either loss. Ultimately, this happened on my watch and it was my decision to use them. In this case, we just didn't have the time or experience with these employees to turn it around. The root cause may have been not interviewing the employees before making a blanket hire of all of them. I'll never know if we could have stopped the election, but my choice to hire without talking to them was a bad one.

We also erred by not making a better effort to drive our culture into the new acquisition swiftly and assertively. We did a below average job of telling our new employees about us, our company, and our culture. We didn't tell stories of how we do things or the way we think. We didn't exemplify our culture enough with our own actions. All in all, we did a perfunctory job of telling them who we were and then just went about our business.

As a result, we suffered through seven years of union hell: endless contract negotiations, numerous charges filed with the NLRB, and a strike. The worst part was a relationship with the drivers that was always adversarial and sometimes borderline hostile. It permeated throughout the company, infecting even good-natured employees. It was agonizing to see this happen to my managers in Indianapolis and to our company as a whole. We had prided ourselves as a great employer with excellent relationships with our employees. This was the antithesis of our entire value system and long-term goals.

NLRB Primer

A short aside is worthwhile here. The National Labor Relations Board (NLRB) was created by the National Labor Relations Act (NLRA) of 1935. The year itself should tell you something about this law. It was created in a time when some employers were less than caring about their employees. Maybe they paid too little or no overtime or provided job conditions that were unhealthy or unsafe. I'm sure they were abusive in other ways too. Today, if you want to stay in business, that seems virtually impossible to do. Recruiting and retaining quality employees is probably the most significant challenge for all employers today. You must be a good (or great) employer if you want to succeed or even just stay in business.

The NLRB is a political entity. It tends to be swayed based on what party controls the White House. Eight years of either party can produce big swings. We were in the middle of the Obama administration for eight years and got beat up pretty good by the NLRB. At one point, googling me produced a top result of my labor dealings—written by the NLRB. They once featured me in their newsletter and called me a "bad actor," the worst you can be called by the NLRB, which I wore as a badge. Here is why:

Our drivers were represented by the Teamsters. We would negotiate according to the law, but that doesn't guarantee a contract. When the Teamsters came to believe we would not agree to *any* contract (which wasn't true), they began to file Unfair Labor Practice charges (ULPs). These ranged from failing to give an employee a position he said he didn't want to moving the coffee pot location. (I am not kidding.) These charges are filed by the union with the NLRB for potential certification by the NLRB Regional Director. (During our time in Indianapolis, he never failed NOT to certify a union charge against us.) After that, if we didn't agree with the charge, a hearing is held before an Administrative Law Judge or ALJ–an employee of the NLRB, not an elected official. The ALJ hears the case and makes a decision at his sole discretion. As you might expect, the ALJ ruled against us every time.

More nonsense follows. Your next option is to file an appeal with the NLRB in Washington, which is decided by a five-member board appointed by the President. The board is usually biased towards the party of the President. During our time, they always ruled against us. Lose there and the next step is to file an appeal with a federal appeals court. This is finally where you should get a normal, objective, and fair reading of the case. This is true except that, in an appeal, you cannot introduce new evidence or testimony. One can only appeal what is in the existing record. Unfortunately, the record of the case is decided largely by the ALJ, including their thoughts on whether witnesses or evidence are credible. Hence, my reputation as a bad actor was born.

If you lose the appeal at the federal appeals court level, theoretically you can appeal to the U.S. Supreme Court. Here, unless you are a huge company, or your issue is truly impacting companies across the country, your case will not be selected and heard.

So, the bottom line is you can spend a lot of time and money pursuing justice when the NLRB receives a charge against you, but the likelihood of winning is against you. My experience included one case that took over six years and $400,000 to get to a final decision and settlement. We spent that time and money because we (foolishly) believed we could win and the issues we pursued would impart precedents on compensation and work rules for the foreseeable future. We should have saved the money.

We persevered through those seven years of union hell, but it wasn't all bad. Economically, we spent on attorney fees about half of the wage and benefit increases that were in our last offer to the union. That was a good economic outcome, I reasoned, but it amazed me to think that the union couldn't do math. The drivers they represented—purportedly to help raise wages and benefits—were convinced by the union not to take our offer because the union was standing firm on a signing bonus. They wanted us to pay a bonus to each employee for signing the contract. I disagreed on principle and they walked away. The simple math indicated that the drivers would have made up the bonus in less than two years. While it turned out economically good for us via wages and benefits, I still believe we lost productivity due to the continued strain. I also believed they deserved the higher wages, which were commensurate with the market.

The End and the New Beginning

The end started slowly. The drivers that were union leaders and diehards slowly went away. A few were fired but most simply quit. In general, we were fighting ULPs by the ones that were fired and ended up paying some to go away. At the end, the few drivers left who were present from the beginning forgot what they were fighting for, and more recent hires didn't care to hear old war stories.

We soon began to get questions about the union and why they hadn't received wage increases since we bought the company. We explained that the union represented them, and we couldn't do anything without negotiating with the union. It didn't make much sense to the newer guys and their questions became more detailed. At that point, legally, we could only answer so much but we could tell them to call the NLRB for more information. Eventually, it led to 100 percent of the drivers signing a petition to vote on union representation. The election day was set, but two weeks before it arrived, the union sent the NLRB a letter withdrawing representation. It meant they didn't want an election and would just quit. It was a huge victory—even bigger than when the union didn't show up for the election.

We waited about a month to make sure there were no shenanigans from the union or the NLRB and then held an employee meeting. I congratulated them on their decision to represent themselves and work directly with us to make our company great. Then I announced wage increases and better benefits—at the level of our employees in Ohio. Everyone seemed shocked; I don't think they expected change so quickly. After explaining how the new benefits would work and the paperwork they needed to fill out, I looked them over. I couldn't have been prouder and happier with any group of employees.

I thought that I really didn't know many of them very well, so I decided to start changing that right then and there. I said, "I want everyone to get to know each other and that includes me. Let's start right now." I walked to the first row and started with the first guy on the right. "Introduce yourself to everyone, let us know where you are from and something about yourself." We heard all kinds of interesting things, some heartfelt and others humorous. The meeting ended with a lot of smiles.

I still remember talking to one driver, Anthony Fisher. He was a big guy. I'm 6' 5" and 200 lbs. but felt tiny. He was about 6' 10" and 350 lbs. He walked up to me and shook my little hand with his big paw. He said thank you and told me what a great company and group of guys I had. He looked awfully tough, but his eyes and words were kind and honest. It made my day.

As I walked away from talking to Anthony, I asked his manager, "Tell me about the big guy over there, what's his story?" He said, "You mean Big Fish?" He went on to tell me that Tony Fisher aka Big Fish had a hard life growing up: gangs, drugs, living in a dangerous part of town, and more. One time, Tony had told him he had been shot four different times but that he could still do any job. I said, "Wow. What do you say to that?" The manager smiled and said, "I told him he needed to run faster." The funny part of that story is that I knew he was joking with him and he could say that because their relationship was close.

Another reason I'll never forget Tony is the day I announced to this same group that I was selling the company. The new owners were there, and I said a few words and introduced them. Right after the meeting, Big Fish came over to me and just opened his arms and hugged me. My head was smothered in his chest and he squeezed tight. I felt like a little kid being held by his father. He thanked me for the opportunity we gave him and wished me luck.

The last reason is just as special. After I had sold the company, I talked to the manager that ran Indianapolis for me. He caught me up on how things were going with the new owners and told me a lot of guys had said how they missed me and the old days. I laughed and he said, "No, I'm not kidding, they are serious. You know what I just heard? They all pooled their money to buy a lottery ticket for that $250 million drawing, and Tony stood in front of the drivers and said, "Keep your fingers all crossed because we are going to win tonight! And when we win, we going to buy this company and give it back to Jim!"

Decertifying the union in Indianapolis was my last union battle. It was a fitting end to my history with organized labor. In total, I had decertified five unions. As vice president and general manager with my former employer, I had taken over a company with a 100 percent hourly union workforce and left it as 100 percent non-union. I started and kept my Ohio company non-union and finally achieved the same with my Indianapolis company. It was a long road.

On a purely academic basis, I have no problems with or animus against unions. I'm sure they still serve a purpose in some companies. I also know that the choice to have a union represent employees rest solely with the employees. They make that choice. They vote them in or out. It's up to us, as owners and leaders, to earn their confidence and respect so they don't go looking for a union.

While this was a long history to read about, I tell it because it taught me so much about employee relations. My experience with employing people is sprinkled with stories about unions from which I learned important lessons. They have as much to do with being a good employer as they do with the unions themselves. Today, I believe that no company can thrive, or perhaps even survive, without being a good employer.

CHAPTER 9

THE FINE LINE BETWEEN RISKS AND REWARDS

Risk stands out as the most valuable and least considered part of small business decision-making. If entrepreneurs have an Achilles heel, it is in the assessment of risk—the failure to take it into account for all decisions, particularly major ones. Risk is the disrespected stepchild that tags along with reward. Overlooked, ignored, and even disregarded, it is the equal partner to reward but never gets its due. At least sometimes—not until it's too late.

Most of us understand risk when it comes to investments. We know that all investments come with a profile for potential risk and return. Buying stock in a start-up Silicon Valley company is not the same as buying a Treasury Note backed by the U.S. Government. The former is high risk but potentially high reward. You could be buying the next Google or Apple. The return is not easy to estimate but the sky is the limit. The latter is very low risk but relatively low return. In fact, the ultra-low risk profile means that the return is all but guaranteed. It is very predictable. We all get this concept but often do not recognize the same inherent trade-offs in business.

Many business leaders know that risk needs to be considered in the big decisions, so they take time to factor it into their analysis. However, there is risk in just about *every* action you take or fail to take. There can be risk in making capital expenditures, hiring people, pursuing new technology, or shifting a sales focus. Almost anything and everything. Risk analysis may take a few minutes—or days—of gathering information and performing the necessary analysis. Risk also needs to considered not just when identifiable dollars are at play but also when investing time and focus. If most companies say, correctly, that their biggest asset is their people, then their biggest investment and risk is where and how a business directs its focus. It can be just as rewarding and just as risky whether you get this right or wrong.

It's easy to understand the urge to ignore risk in the early years of starting and owning a business. There is a maddening focus on just getting started or getting to a steady state of sales. By nature, entrepreneurs are risk-takers; the early years of a business will accommodate that quite well. It's easier to understand, but it's still not prudent to ignore or pay insufficient attention to risk. In later years, when a business has gained some value and continues to increase this value, there is a natural tendency to consider risk more as a part of major decision-making.

The Easiest Decision Is Not Always the Best

Considering risk is ultra-important in every decision and at every stage of business. It can never be less than an equal partner to reward and sometimes may outweigh it. It should not be *whether* to include risk as part of assessing a decision; it should be *how* to weigh it. Am I willing to accept "X" amount of risk for "Y" reward? Are there other factors in my business that preclude me from taking a certain amount of risk? Likewise, am I able to take on more risk at certain times to seize an opportunity? These questions, and their many variants, are critical to maximizing profit and increasing or preserving the value of your business.

> We had two very successful years as a start-up. Things were going very well, and we had beaten our forecasts and pro forma financial statements. This was not unheard of but still impressive. We were also optimistic about the coming year of business. We had a right to be proud and even confident, but pride and confidence can be enemies too.
>
> The end of the year is when companies like ours typically order trucks for the coming year. We were in a seasonal market where our business of supplying construction projects ran most strongly from April through October. So, it made sense to order trucks late in the year for delivery in the spring when business typically ramps up. I had considered whether it made sense that year to order more trucks to increase our sales (trucks are manufacturing capacity in our industry). The new ones were far from worn out or needing replacement, and we still had an incredible amount

of debt. However, our cash flow was sufficient to cover additional debt, and it seemed that we could grow.

An unfortunate influence probably made up my mind. Our banks were happy with our results and asked whether we were planning additional capital expenditures for the coming year. The conversation indicated they were essentially pre-approving a loan to buy more trucks. The encouragement was another boost to our confidence. I weighed the possibility of adding more trucks to our fleet and whether the market would continue to help us grow or whether our competition might take exception to that via lower pricing and more pressure in the market.

I decided that our two years of experience was solid enough, our sales projections were encouraging, and we would order ten more trucks—an additional 22 percent increase in capacity after just two years. Growth of that magnitude may not be unusual for some industries, but for a mature industry like construction materials and in a low growth state like Ohio, it was a big move.

Spring began that year and the ten new trucks started coming in. We stayed busy and put them to use but never seemed to be fully utilizing them. It was as if we went from 90 percent utilization of forty-five trucks to 80 percent utilization of fifty-five trucks. By the end of that year, I guessed that we over-ordered new trucks by three times. We could have easily done the same volume and only bought three new trucks.

In retrospect, it was an aggressive bullseye to aim for, and it was unrealistic and risky. We were overly confident of our ability, and available financing tilted our decision towards a harder-to-hit target than we should have settled on. Early in the life of a new business, it can be intoxicating to think of hitting lofty sales growth goals. However, careful consideration of the correct bullseye is still needed. We could have used a dose of reality and patience with our aspirations.

It's also hard to forecast business. The decision to add capacity or determine what capacity utilization will be is not an exact science. It is a gray area for our industry but not so much that you can't see most of the trees in the forest. It took us another three years to garner enough business that our capacity was being utilized at the rate we achieved in the second year. We shouldered additional debt and laid out precious cash to make payments on trucks that we didn't need. It wasn't a disaster, but it was a poor decision and a waste of resources.

In making that decision, I don't remember considering risk nearly enough. I do remember considering reward. Risk is a lot like asking "what if" questions and considering the range of effects of a specific decision. How much more can I sell if I increase capacity? How much more profit would I make? If there was anything close to risk considered in this situation, it was: "What would happen if we don't buy trucks and someone else takes this additional business?" It was a reasonable thought but still not enough to balance the analysis.

Hitting my bullseye was the prime consideration of this decision. Missing the bullseye crossed my mind but never hitting any part of the target did not. Imagine shooting ten arrows (think trucks) and missing the whole target with seven of them. Not a good day at the archery range! Taking dead aim is one of my favorite concepts and understanding how to hit the bullseye, with all that goes into it, is of prime importance to any business. No less important than considering the chance of hitting the bullseye is the chance of missing it.

Every day, risk assessment creeps into (or, more accurately, out of) ordinary business. Vigilance is needed to continue to assess and reassess as needed. When the "as needed" part is not obvious, remember to revisit it on some sort of periodic basis, depending on likelihood of change and the magnitude of inherent risk. Managing risk is not just an insurance term but applicable to all parts of your business.

Risks Within Markets

In supplying concrete to construction projects, a company can focus on one or several parts of the construction industry. At one end, there is residential work that might consist of sidewalks, patios, and driveways. It also includes foundations for houses and concrete floors found in basements and garages. These are important to the owner but, frankly, do not have much risk to a company like ours. Theoretically, a house could fall in if the concrete foundation fails, but the reality is that most concrete foundations for houses are overdesigned. Driveways may have issues where the surface flakes off or peels away. However, in most residential construction, the failures are minor, easy to fix, and very rarely result in a huge remediation cost. Think about replacing a piece of sidewalk. You jack hammer it up and pour it back with new concrete. There is little cost and no risk of catastrophic failure or loss of life.

At the other end of the spectrum is commercial and industrial construction. This could be a skyscraper, a hotel, an interstate bridge, or a runway at your airport. Concrete failures at these project sites can be catastrophic. While loss of life is seldom the result (the failed concrete is almost always caught before the structure, whatever it is, is put into use by the public), repair costs can be geometrically higher than the original construction. Think about replacing the concrete in a bridge or parking garage. These are complex, highly engineered structures. Think about the foundation of a skyscraper with seventy floors of building on top of it, or the top floor of the skyscraper hundreds of feet in the air. The ramifications of failure—and therefore overall risk—are significantly higher in this type of construction than the sidewalk in front of your house.

In my industry, when you sell concrete, you sell it in cubic yards. When this unit of measure appears on management reports or financial statements, it is the same unit of sales—no matter where it went, what it costs, or how much risk was involved. At a basic level, my sales and operations people talked in terms of how many units sold each day, week, and month. While complexity of certain projects might be discussed or compared, risk was never a primary part of the conversation. It should have been and was eventually incorporated on a regular basis.

The Owner Is in Charge of Risk Management

Throughout my career, I found that considering risk was often left up to me. I was the custodian of this part of my business and no amount of talking about it ever led to me delegating it to others. If it was to be considered, it was up to me. On a good day, I might be able make sure others thought some about it too. During the recession, I found I had to be even more diligent.

Our industry often prices concrete by calculating raw material costs and then adding a fixed number of dollars to arrive at a price to bid or charge. It is different than marking up materials by a certain percentage. The concept is rooted in the fact that the fixed part represents what we have left over to manufacture and deliver concrete, including overhead and profit. While raw material costs may vary by 10-200 percent, the fixed part tends to vary only 5-15 percent. It is logical when you think about it, since profit is in the fixed part, varying far less than the raw materials.

I tended to manage our sales function by giving the sales manager some parameters regarding volume, price, margins, and other relevant items and then let him manage the process. I told him the "what" but not the "how." He would be able to bid most projects, up to a certain size, using these parameters as a guide. He would also have authority to alter prices within a relevant range based on factors such as market, customers, or meeting a competitor's price.

During the depths of the recession, I had more frequent conversations with my sales manager regarding sales and bidding. These were always about how many units we were selling and at what margins, along with other qualitative aspects. However, these conversations seemed less about what product we were selling and the type of project. We were consumed with survival-mode thinking, me included. Over time, I noticed a trend in the market and in our pricing. Sidewalk concrete was going for the same margin as skyscraper concrete. A patio was priced like a bridge on the highway. All margins had fallen, but the more technically difficult work, and therefore the higher-risk work, had fallen quite a bit more. Those margins had begun to approach the margins of the simpler, lower-risk work.

While we had a premier reputation for quality and service with the most difficult specification concrete, more competitors had invaded this space as other parts of the construction market experienced the downturn. As more competitors began bidding these projects, the price naturally started to fall. Luckily, our reputation often afforded us a chance to match a lower price and still win the bid. This strategy amounted to meeting the competitor's price and keeping them from supplying what was usually a loyal customer. I let this philosophy go unchecked for too long and eventually our margins had eroded all the way to the sidewalk concrete level.

I talked to my sales manager and had him pull a multi-year history of these commercial and industrial projects. It confirmed what I had begun to sense. Our backlog was becoming dominated by much lower-margin work. While very difficult times may call for a change in strategy to maintain sales, the margins for these sales did not justify our position. We needed to make a change.

As we considered what that change would look like, we also took a closer look at which customers caused us to incur more costs. This might be due to additional raw materials, transportation, or other service-related costs. Some customers appeared to do this sporadically while others were habitual. In the same way that different types of concrete were riskier in their profitability, the same was true for customers. For several months, I worked closer and more often with our sales manager on how to price in this new environment. I modified the parameters I gave him on pricing and shifted his focus to customers that were more predictable and less risk prone, and on products with margins that balanced complexity and/or risk. Overall, our conversations were quantitative regarding margins but also qualitative regarding risk. I focused on the likelihood of additional costs and even large remediation to limit our downside and specialty products where we could still attain superior margins.

Eventually, we began to shift the type of work and type of customers we targeted. While we never strayed from our commercial and industrial roots, we methodically parred down our reliance on it and did so with risk-adjusted analysis of our sales. The bottom line was we were finally focusing our sales effort on products and customers where we could balance margins with risks.

This was a case of where our aim didn't change but our arrows had begun to drift from the bullseye. Even though we were missing the bullseye, hitting the target was initially enough to not trigger alarms. However, our arrows continued to drift further and further out, to the next circle out and then the next, until they were likely to miss the target altogether.

It may be most difficult to recognize that the environment is causing you to miss your bullseye when the change happens slowly and over time. In this case, it was not perceptible in the short-term as these were small, incremental changes. Over time, trends get noticed but it can be frustrating in retrospect. No one likes to lose critical time by not adjusting their aim and by not shooting straight at the bullseye. The lesson here was to remain ever vigilant in identifying changes and tracking trends and then being nimble and responsive to address those changes.

When Risk Is Your Friend

Risk can also be an ally, serving as a differentiator between several bidders for the same project and offering the chance to increase margins well above average. Risk can drive some companies away from bidding on a project or, if they do, to raising their bid so high as to be uncompetitive. It can also serve to influence the buyers. Perceiving that there are significant differences in the risk of buying from one company versus another may lead to a project award to the less risky supplier. In other words, if a buyer believes that there is higher risk of problems, or even your competitor's failure to supply product, it can lead to awards of work—even if your pricing is higher.

My management team spent the entire life of my company determined to differentiate ourselves from our competitors. Most of the time, it was intentional work towards this goal. We developed capabilities with an eye to providing additional value. This included specialized equipment, personnel training and certifications, or research and development. Sometimes it was done in response to an upcoming project, and sometimes it was done just to have in our arsenal. I often thought of it as trying to have as many tools as possible in our toolbox. You might not always need each one every day, but they can come in handy when you do need them. This was the case when one of the most challenging technical projects came up for bid.

After we had been in business for almost a decade, a very high-profile project was to be built in Cincinnati. It would require the highest strength concrete ever produced in the area. The specification was for strengths commonly found in the tallest buildings in the country—typical for one hundred-story buildings in New York or Chicago but not for the Midwest. The tallest buildings in Cincinnati and every other nearby major city was less than fifty stories.

The project specifications were very demanding. To produce and deliver this concrete would require far more attention than what was typically produced in the area. It generated a lot of talk among contractors and suppliers in the weeks before the bid was due. While contractors are often consumed with the methods and means to build a structure, most of the conversation was turning to who could produce this concrete or whether it could be produced at all. Ultra-high strength concrete production is dependent largely on the quality of the aggregate raw materials. If local aggregates were not suitable, then much more costly aggregate would have to be imported.

I could tell from these conversations that our competitors were struggling with the dilemma. There was not time to appropriately test the raw materials before the bid, so their waking hours were plagued with unknowns. For my company, those unknowns created a competitive advantage. We had conducted a research test program years before to investigate this very thing. We had no way of knowing whether it would be directly useful one day (or at all), but we had proceeded out of professional curiosity. We wanted to know more about the limits of local materials at the time, and how to successfully design and manufacture such products. With that past investigation, we knew for a fact we could produce the required product with local materials. Now, that curiosity was going to pay off.

Several contractors contacted me personally, wanting to go straight to the top for answers on whether we could produce this product. Knowing that my competitors were expressing concern, I remained coy, not wanting to tip my hand. The week of the bid, I told one contractor, "Yeah, we've looked over the specs and they are a bear. I doubt many people even know how to read this thing. We are still discussing it but hope to have a proposal to you at bid time. I think we can put something together." I was trying to accomplish three things, knowing that contractors are not always the best friend they portray themselves to be, and prone to sharing too much with competing suppliers. First, it was possible some competitors might guess that the product could not be manufactured without importing raw materials. This would influence them to raise prices dramatically to cover the extra costs. Second, I didn't want the market to know that we had the knowledge and experience to design and manufacture this product according to specifications. I'd rather have my competitors think everyone is in the same boat and therefore not be tempted to lower their prices based on a guess that it was possible to manufacture with local materials. And finally, I did not want the contractors to try and bring a supplier from outside the market to produce for this project. It was all a tightrope walk: give them some idea that we are concerned but not so much that they look for outsiders to assist them with a bid.

We finalized our proposal by bid day. I knew it would be a challenge, even with our technical advantage. We increased our costs for management and oversight of the project, as well as a dedicated mobile quality-control laboratory staffed with our own certified technicians on the project site. This was something we owned, certified people we had, and could not be matched by any of our competitors. Our final numbers looked crazy high, but I was confident we could convince any contractor that we were the logical choice—and maybe the only choice.

After the project was awarded to the successful bidding contractor, we met with them to discuss our bid. Our presentation was professional, covering every aspect of their needs. It also anticipated some needs they hadn't considered but could assign value to, such as the mobile Q-C Lab we included. It went very well. We later received a request to reduce our pricing. There wasn't much explanation except to say it was needed in order to award us the project. I didn't think much about this request; they were simply shopping for a better price. I was confident that we gave them the best proposal, so we held firm and waited. It didn't take long; they called the next day and awarded us the project.

Though not nearly as often as I'd like, we have been rewarded appropriately for our expertise, knowledge, and experience. This time it was not just a project award but also one with premium pricing and margins. It also came with the prestige of providing concrete on such a high-profile and demanding project.

This was also an affirmation that knowing one's industry and business is critical. Continuing to learn more about what your industry can do keeps you abreast of the latest trends and how far the envelope is being pushed. This is especially valuable when those envelope limits are an opportunity to show that you know these limits and can address them like any other cutting-edge organization. Knowing our industry inside and out, and what our company was capable of, proved to be a worthwhile investment.

We were rewarded because we prepared for such opportunities without knowing if or when they would appear. We could not have known that we would one day have to prepare to hit a bullseye that never previously existed in our market. We were prepared because, initially, it was a way gaining expertise beyond what our market required. It would benefit our business in other ways. That benefit comes from having the knowledge and confidence that we can hit all bullseyes; therefore, hitting "everyday" targets seems like less of a challenge or effort. It gave our people and our customers confidence in us. It also gave us access to opportunities that were out of our competitors' reach.

The Risk of Selling Out—Or Not

Risk also played a critical role in deciding to sell my company. Price, timing, and a changing market played big roles, of course, but I used risk to make the final decision. In fact, it was more front-and-center in my decision-making process than at any other time in my career.

> Leading up to the selling of my business, I considered several factors. Many things were swirling through my mind, but the final decision revolved around the expected return on investment (ROI) of two things. Either I would keep my business or take the proceeds and invest them. Each choice had attending risks. These were not hard to calculate, albeit with expected ranges rather than an exact number. I had seventeen years of history running the business. I felt comfortable estimating the continuing return during normal business cycles for the next ten to twenty years. The stock and bond markets were even easier to estimate. While you can never predict the next downturn or recession, or the severity and

duration, you can forecast with some confidence what this may look like for stocks and bonds over the long run.

Risk is different. For stocks and bonds, I felt the risk was low over the long term. I was fifty-four and would probably live another thirty years. Over those thirty-plus years, there seemed to be very little risk with a balanced portfolio of stocks and bonds. Like a typical investor, I would change the balance to more and more bonds over time to reflect my age, needs, and decreasing acceptance of risk. Obviously, I didn't want to be seventy-five and have much risk, so my portfolio would reflect that as I grew older.

My business was different. It was not a mix of hundreds of stocks and bonds and did not track the national market or any index. It was a mature industry business, not very big relative to the national and international companies that dominated the industry. It was located in a part of the U.S. not known for growth. It was also subject to vagaries I could not control or anticipate. For example, my former employer was bought out by a very wealthy businessman with a reputation for being a tough competitor. This dramatically changed the market and the risk of continuing to operate my business with historical sales and profits.

I couldn't quantify the risk of continuing to own my business but tried to reconcile its risk factor relative to the stock and bond markets. In my mind, continuing to own my business had a factor of "X" times more risk than stocks and bonds. Maybe it was 10 percent or maybe it was 200 percent. Clearly, I needed to make a determination of what that was.

When it came time to make my decision, I made a guess at what the risk of continuing ownership was relative to selling now and owning stocks and bonds. To evaluate this,

I came up with three scenarios: 1) Sell now for $X, 2) Sell later for 90 percent of $X, and 3) Sell later for 120 percent of $X. I assigned each scenario a likelihood of happening and defined what "later" was. (I actually defined "later" a few different ways and re-ran the analysis with each.) None of this was scientific, but I created a spreadsheet for my own combination of "what ifs." The best case was out-earning stocks and bonds and selling for more than my current offer. The worst case was the opposite of under-earning and selling for less. I pegged the best case at far less likely than the worst case, and the iterations in between swung the decision towards selling. It ended being a no brainer because I had considered risk. Without any such consideration, it might have been a toss-up or swung the other way. It also might have been a huge mistake.

There is no doubt that different businesses have different risk considerations. I can think of a lot of ways that risk can be present. Whether you are weighing investments, business operation strategies, or even whether to sell your business, risk should never be the ignored elephant in the room. It should be considered carefully and quantified as much as possible. Even if it seems like a guessing game, take the time to make as full an analysis as possible as to what risk means and how it figures into the equation.

The spreadsheet I created for my business sale included upsides and downsides, but also accounted for swings in value caused by the economy. This meant I had to consider the severity, duration, and frequency of these swings. It was not overly complicated, and it made me think hard about the impact of my decision. In the end, the bullseye became very clear, almost as if I was half the distance to the target (and therefore twice as confident with my decision.) After eighteen years in business, and all my effort to grow my business's value, risk was an equal partner to reward in making my decision to sell.

I also made sure to treat my business objectively. I had to see it as a single owned asset—but by far the largest I owned. More precisely, it meant I had virtually all my net worth tied up in this one asset. It was like having a stock portfolio of only one stock. Even if it was a quality company with a long record of stable earnings, owning only one stock was the opposite of diversification and minimizing risk. Therefore, keeping my business would mean accepting a much higher degree of risk.

The consideration of risk in selling or keeping my business hinged on the priorities of my family's well-being and security. This meant my decision could very well be the largest determinant of my family priorities. For me, this might include support for college tuition, apartments, cars, first house down payments, and a long list of possible unanticipated expenses, like serious health issues. None of these go on indefinitely, and some may never happen, but it was reasonable to assume that many of them would occur, and I wanted to be financially able to handle them.

In the end, this was the overwhelming influence on my decision to sell. The risk of losing some or even a large chunk of my business's value was not worth the potential upside. When a more than reasonable offer to buy my company was presented to me, my consideration of family and risk made my decision an easy one.

CHAPTER 10

WORKING OUT WHAT YOUR BUSINESS IS WORTH

Everyone wonders what their business is worth. Even publicly traded companies will have opinions about whether their stock price is under or overvaluing their company. (According to them, it is always undervalued.) Private company owners should have a method, or at least a philosophy, of how they estimate this. However, just like an estimate for your house, you don't know what it is really worth until someone buys it.

The importance and usefulness of estimating your business's worth should drive several decisions, not just whether to sell it. This includes decisions about capital expenditures or acquisitions. It may help you decide whether to expand into new markets or even exit low performing ones. In all cases, it is part of the equation as you decide how a decision or strategy will impact the return on your investment. Your investment *is* your business. Your decisions will affect how much you earn on your investment (i.e. your business).

Useful Valuation Concepts

As CEO, increasing the value of your business is a primary concern. Therefore, the valuation method you use is important. It will guide most of your actions on a macro level. Here are some common measures used for valuations.

EBITDA

In my industry, as in many others, valuations for acquisitions are often made based on a "multiple of EBITDA," which stands for Earnings Before Interest, Taxes, Depreciation, and Amortization. Using some number times EBITDA isn't the only way a buyer will calculate a valuation, but it is the way to compare different valuations or deals. With comparisons, the actual dollars being paid doesn't matter as much as the multiple. Let's take a quick look at what EBITDA means and follow it with two examples:

» **Earnings** means Net Income, or sometimes Profit. It is the last line of your financial statement and is what's left after all expenses have been deducted from revenue. Don't confuse this with Gross Income or Operating Income or anything that comes before the last line.

» **Before** means you are adding back items to Earnings. It may seem obvious what "before" means, but to be concise, think of it as a "+" sign.

» **Interest** is all interest paid on loans you have, including vehicles, real estate, equipment, and lines of credit.

» **Taxes** are all those paid on income. It should not include taxes paid on fuel, real estate, et cetera.

» **Depreciation** is the allocation of the purchase price of fixed assets over their useful life. If you book depreciation and have it on your income statement, then that's it.

» **Amortization** is like depreciation. It is a charge taken over time for something you bought that is not a fixed asset and you can't physically put your hands on it. Examples are goodwill, intellectual property, a marketing name, et cetera.

Here are some simple examples:

» Company A has $10 million in revenue, Net Income of $1 million, and EBITDA of $2 million. They are paid $13 million for their company. The "multiple" is **6.5X** or 6.5 multiplied by $2 million.

» Company B has $50 million in revenue, Net Income of $6 million, and EBITDA of $15 million. They are paid $75 million for their company. The "multiple" is **5X** or 5 multiplied by $15 million.

It could be said that Company A was paid a premium compared to B because of the higher multiple even though the total price was much less. Further analysis may yield a number of other comparisons, but the EBITDA multiple tends to take the headline. Almost everybody valuing a business in any industry will talk about this, although it is hardly the whole analysis.

Discounted Cash Flow

Discounted Cash Flow (DCF) is a method used by more sophisticated financial executives. Put simply, it is a forecasted financial statement over several years that considers how much cash you take in minus how much you pay out. So, besides forecasting sales and expenses, you might take into account how much you spend on capital expenditures or other cash outlays. Then, the real exercise is calculating how much the value of this multi-year forecast is today when added up using a Discount Rate for the future cash flows over a stated number of years. The Discount Rate is like an interest rate but is used to discount future years' cash flow. The concept is the same as realizing that $1 is worth more today than $1 five years from now. Also, the same as a savings account example of $1 deposited at your bank today in a 5 percent savings account will be worth $1.05 in a year and $1.28 in five years. Working in the opposite direction, a forecasted profit of $1.28 million five years from now is worth $1 million today in a DCF analysis.

DCF analysis also considers risk. In the above example, I decided the risk of putting my $1 in a bank was 0 percent. In other words, I was at no risk of losing my $1 over that year. The bank was solid, and the amount was very small. Not all investments should be viewed that way. In fact, no investment is truly risk-free so there needs to be an assignment of a risk factor. This will reduce the return calculated by DCF by that risk factor each year. The risk factor can also be thought of as a targeted rate of return. If 5 percent is risk free in a bank, then you might want 10–20 percent or even more for an investment in a business.

Here's how that works. In the example above, we discounted the $1.28 million by 5 percent each year to arrive at $1 million today. With risk factored in, you might want to discount at 15 percent. This would be your targeted return. If I want my business to grow in value at 15 percent per year, then you use that rate to discount the cash flow. So, our $1.28 five years from now, discounted at 15 percent per year, is worth $0.64 today—a big difference!

Your analysis would also require a duration for the calculation. It might be from five years to ten or fifteen, depending on the type of business and its future operational reliability. The longer out you go, the less additional value you can expect each additional year to add to the total.

There is more to say about DCF, but hopefully the stories below will give an idea of how it works. It's worth noting that DCF analysis is often used in conjunction with an Internal Rate of Return (IRR) calculation. This is an analysis by which a set of assumptions regarding cash flows indicate a rate of return, very similar to an annualized ROI.

Some Valuation Deviations

The above methods represent what are commonly used to calculate the value of profitable private businesses. There are other methods, some used primarily by public companies, but these methods outline the basics for many if not most private entities. Having said that, there is no shortage of opinions as to which is better—and some alternatives.

When I began to seriously consider selling my business, I also began to consider what value it would bring in a sale and whether I would consider that value fair. Throughout my career, I had numerous conversations about valuing a business in my industry, most recently in my peer group. Rumors and current events fueled these conversations but there were also discussions about internal analysis.

One of my best friends in the industry, a well-respected and successful CEO, always presented an impassioned view. His take, and his company's formula for a bonus structure was predicated on calculating Return on Net Assets (RONA), using a simple formula. He explained it this way, "We only look at RONA. That's the only way it makes sense to us. I'm tired of all the talk about Cash Flow and EBITDA. That stuff doesn't matter. It's about Net Income, that's what you really make, and how much of a return that is on your net assets, the stuff you own to run the business." That made some sense, but I pressed him on it. "Jerry, I get what you are saying, but Net Income can be distorted by depreciation, by how much debt you carry, and your tax structure. It doesn't have a way of being comparable across companies like EBITDA." He wouldn't budge and brought up the difference with capital expenditures. He said, "EBITDA doesn't consider reinvesting in the company. Net Income is the only real number, and to a large degree it considers this reinvestment because depreciation is a real cost, not something to be added back."

We respectfully agreed to disagree. There were pluses and minuses to each argument, but he wasn't going to change no matter what. While I firmly believe EBITDA is the most consistent measure across a wide variety of companies, I respected that his company embraced a measure and stuck with it. At least they were consistent, and it would work for things like a bonus based on profits like Net Income.

Another friend believed that only Discounted Cash Flow (DCF) was realistic. His logic was simple too. He elaborated, "DCF is the only way to go. It is the only analysis that uses actual cash, which is the only thing that is real. It is the only way to keep score." He went on, "DCF takes the real cash you make from operations, pays all the taxes and interest, pays for new CAPEX, and here is the most important part: it takes into account the time-value of money and risk." Now he was talking my language, but I still had a problem.

I told him, "I agree with everything you said, but DCF is hard to compare across different companies and through several years because it has a lot of inputs and moving parts. This is especially true if the analysis period varies or if risk changes. And those are big drivers of the final value number." My point was that to compare, even internally, more than one company or one-time horizon, there would be several or maybe many variables making good comparisons difficult.

My final comment to both was essentially the same. Valuations have a market component. Therefore, you must be able measure across different sizes, geographies, and time periods. It is one thing to have a measure used internally to gauge growth or success, but to derive a market valuation, you must have a comparable tool. And "comparable tools" by their nature may not necessarily be the most accurate for a given situation, but they are the most consistent.

Most would agree that a valuation calculation is an important tool to use whether you are buying or selling a business. I would add that it is equally important throughout the life of any business that you own. It is no less important than wanting to know what interest rate your savings account is paying or how much the stock you own went up last year. Regardless of the precise accuracy of the estimated valuation, it would be irresponsible not to go through the process of calculating it regularly.

My last thought on this subject is to suggest that, whatever method you use, it would be useful to be as consistent as possible. Deciphering year-over-year differences and long-term trends is difficult enough without changing valuation methods. If there isn't a compelling reason to change your valuation method, then stick with one method over time. If you do feel like a different method makes more sense, go back and re-calculate prior years so you have a historic apples-to-apples comparison.

What's Your Return?

Whether analyzing the valuation of your business for a plan to sell or just tracking it to see how you are doing, a final step should include calculating the return on your investment. If you are like me and have 90 percent of your net worth in one place, then you will want to know what your return *is*. Just like knowing what performance a stock had in one year, three years, five years, and ten years, you want to track this. You will probably not make decisions based on only one year but more likely on five or ten years, or possibly on having seen an emerging trend.

Here are some thoughts on return, or what you are making on this investment (also known as your business.)

Return

Return on Investment (ROI) is a commonly used, easy to understand term. It is what you are earning on your investment. In a savings account at a bank, it is the interest rate. For my $100 deposit, I might receive 2 percent interest or $2 per year. Two percent is the ROI. For a stock that I bought five years ago at $100 and sold today for $128, the return is 28 percent. The difference is the savings example is an annual return and the stock example is a TOTAL return. Neither is better than the other. They are simply different, and both are useful to an investor.

When selling a business, the total return is frequently considered since it is often over many years that you are considering your investment. It doesn't mean that the annual return isn't important; in fact, it is more important in many instances. To consider the annual (or annualized) return, there needs to be an additional calculation, as we did in the DCF discussion.

This additional calculation usually involves an analysis that yields the Internal Rate of Return (IRR). This considers the total return and the number of years the investment is held and gives you an annualized rate. In the stock example above, a $100 investment that sells for $128 five years later yields an annualized return of 5 percent.

ROI and IRR are two of the most important concepts to consider when selling your business. If I am made an offer to sell my business, I must ask myself, "Is this a good price?" and be able to answer *why* it is. This also applies to everyday business. Before investing in a new piece of machinery, I need to assess the cost, the return, and the risk. How much will it cost? This is the easiest calculation of the three: I received three quotes, this is the best quote, and so that is what it costs.

The return is a little more involved. Now you must estimate what it costs to operate the machinery and how much more sales it will bring in (or how much it will lower costs). The former estimate is usually straightforward, but the latter may have nuances or unknowns. Estimating additional sales might take into account questions like "How much more sales?", "At what margins are the new sales?", "How will new sales affect my current customer base?", and "How will new sales affect my market and competitors?" Similar questions arise if the aim is to lower costs.

Balancing Return and Risk

Once a return is arrived at, then risk must be assessed. This is the grayest part of the equation but at least as important. In our DCF and ROI discussion, risk and return often get lumped together into a single discount rate or rate of return. It is the simplest methodology. For example, you might desire a 5 percent return, but the risk of a certain investment demands an additional 10 percent. So, the overall rate—return and risk together—would be 15 percent.

In my own business, I looked at the company's value and investments in capital expenditures differently. When considering a new investment in equipment for manufacturing capacity, I might consider how confident I was in my additional sales estimate and the likelihood that my forecast would be accurate. I often ran into this analytical challenge. Here was one episode.

Six years into my business, I found that our success was more than we expected. We were increasing sales well above the average market growth rate. We had added more capacity by buying more trucks and still were operating at nearly 100 percent capacity every day. With a consistent sales trend and no additional capacity available, it was an obvious choice to consider adding capacity.

My sales manager brought this up towards the end of the sixth year. He was a typical sales type—focused on sales almost to the exclusion of anything else. He was driven primarily by how many units we were selling. This is not to say he was oblivious to margins, loyalty, repeat customers, or service, but certainly focused on sales units.

He offered his analysis for the future. He had taken our unit sales and net income for the most recent year and divided this by the number of trucks we currently operated. This resulted in unit sales and profit per truck. Based on this estimate, he felt we should buy twenty more trucks next year. In turn, our unit sales and profits would go up by the per-truck profit number he calculated times twenty, the number of trucks he thought we should add. It was simple and to some degree logical. Since he took the time to do this, I took time to go over a few other things we might add to the analysis.

I asked him to tell me how he came up with the twenty new trucks figure. He said, based on our past six years of growth, forecasts he had read for the coming year's construction activity, and discussions with current customers, he felt this was a good number. "Ten trucks would be safe, but we have the opportunity to grab more market share and I know I can sell the additional volume." I liked his attitude and optimism, but I wasn't on board with the analysis yet.

I asked him to investigate a few more things and also to consider some possible risks. The additional information requests were centered around finding more sources of data and analyzing the accuracy of the data sources in prior years. In our industry, both associations and public companies publish forecasts. I gave him some names and said we should consider how well their prior forecasts correlated with our past performance. All of this would handle my quantitative curiosity.

The risks I mentioned were more qualitative things to consider. Over several years prior to this point, there had been shifts in our market. Several companies had made acquisitions; several others had faded or gone out of business. This competitive dynamic shift had benefited us and helped us grow. We may have positioned ourselves well to pick up this "extra" growth, but there was no evidence that this trend would continue. There was a limit to how much consolidation could occur in the future.

I was also concerned about how our purchase of extra capacity would play out in the market. We would still have to convince more customers to buy from us and win more competitive bids. If the market did not grow sufficiently, pricing for customers and competitive bid projects would come under pressure. This almost always came with an influence over the entire market, not just a particular customer or project. In other words, pricing on all our work could suffer.

This was the hardest concept to talk about in terms of its effect on our business. Too much capacity in the market can be devastating. Some competitors react quickly and start cutting prices. It takes about one second to cut a price, but it can take years to recover that price cut. Our market had been healthy; prices and margins had been increasing along with volume. However, I knew only a fool would think it would go on or go up forever.

My sales manager's data search came back with an interesting set of new data. While all the forecasts were up, there was more diversity in how much and in what segments. I viewed the new dispersion of data as a sign that things were not quite as "steady as she goes" as they were in prior years. Counting on 4-5 percent growth is great, but it rarely continues year after year. This was combined with a wide variety of opinions on where the growth would come from. It was just enough to make me hesitate. I viewed this new information as positive but also adding to our risk.

In the end, it was an exercise in educating my sales manager. He came to understand my view that margins and market stability should be more heavily weighted in our analysis than pure forecasted sales volume. We ended up ordering ten trucks—a healthy increase but not beyond the conservative end of our forecast. I was confident we were not going to give up much market share if we were wrong on the low side. At the same time, we were protected from compounding an overcapacity problem on the high side. Risk was the deciding factor in erring to the conservative side. Our analysis panned out; the additional capacity was absorbed but did not create overcapacity and unnecessary debt.

This example may be more of a case of balancing the right bullseye given the risk of missing our target. The detrimental outcome of missing the bullseye by a lot or even missing the entire target outweighed the potential gain of hitting the bigger payoff bullseye suggested by my sales manager. I wasn't willing to take on that risk. My bullseye was a better bet even if the potential gain might have had a smaller upside.

As for my business as a whole, things were not so easy to decipher. Even so, I tried to always take the time to do the work of evaluating my business's performance and current state of value. Here was my take:

Every year, after we had closed our financial books and I had time to reflect, I would always try to calculate how my investment was doing. As my largest personal asset by far, how was the company doing? I did not involve anyone else with this, nor did it take a lot of time. It was just more of a gut check. I asked, from a very high level, am I doing okay, are there any trends to see, and of course, what has been my return?

On an academic level, my initial investment was $40,000—the actual cash I put into the business. One might say this is what I should base my return on. However, that doesn't work so well when you also borrow a lot of money to start with. I focused more on the year-over-year improvement and the return on current value. (It would not have been prudent to base a decision on the original investment over ten years earlier.)

So, over the course of a year, I would keep articles and other information on valuations of companies in my industry. Some was public and some not. I'd store it in a file, look back at the end of the year and try to assemble an estimate of my company's value. In my case, it usually became a multiple of EBITDA. I would look at other ways of valuing my company but only as a "check number." The one I stuck with was a multiple of EBITDA.

Once I arrived at the company value using the EBITDA calculation, I would use "free cash flow" to calculate return.

The free cash flow I used was Net Income PLUS Depreciation/Amortization MINUS Capital Expenditure (CAPEX). This was what I considered the real cash generated by my business. By dividing free cash flow by the value of my company, I got the return I earned the prior year. It's not perfect, but done over several years, it reveals a meaningful average or trend.

In this way, it is much like the examples of interest earned at your bank on a savings account or how much you earned on a stock investment. Since I had distilled this down to a fairly basic level, I used it to generally compare to what I might have earned on a savings account (relatively risk free) or a bond portfolio (low risk) or a stock portfolio (medium risk). From that, I'd get an idea if the return on keeping and running my business was equal to some other investment and, if so, what was more or less risky.

When I did decide to sell, it was because I felt keeping my business was riskier than selling it and investing in a balanced bond/stock portfolio. While my business could generate higher returns in some years, overall it was not as consistent and had wider return/valuation swings. This meant more risk, particularly as to timing. I looked back and saw valuations go up and down significantly. Some years, acquirers were paying higher multiples for businesses and other years they dropped like a bomb. The additional risk was manifested in not being able to optimally time a future sale. I was risking that I might need or want to sell in a down market. Therefore, the timing of my sale was dictated by a swing in valuations that made keeping my business a much higher risk.

This is the single least-discussed issue among business owners. What is my business worth and when and why should I sell it?

Say that your goal is to retire and generate income equal to your current pay. If so, shouldn't you track this on an annual basis, at least, to see how things are going? You sure would check your bank balance or stock brokerage account more than once a year. The real lesson I learned was to analyze and track how I was doing on the biggest investment I ever had. Even if it was imperfect, I wanted to make an educated guess so I could see how I was doing.

This is the most important bullseye. The biggest decision you will make in your professional life is when to sell your business. Starting it will have seemed relatively easy. Running it will be a passing memory. Selling it will be the realization of all that hard work and confirmation that it was worth it. This process demands tracking that arrow on the way to the bullseye and making adjustments along the way. How else would you treat such a big investment?

CHAPTER 11

MANAGING WITHIN A SHIFTING MARKET

For many business owners, the thought of selling their company may not occur for years or even decades. Often, we are too busy starting, building, growing, or even saving our companies to give much energy to thinking about selling. For others, it may be the process of transferring ownership to the next generation. Multi-generational ownership is fraught with its own perils and there can be a myriad of difficulties in achieving this.

Others, like me, may give it some thought along the way but do not do any formal planning. It may be our age, or the economy, or the fact that our business is a success that keeps us from seriously considering a sale. One might say, "Well, maybe someday, but I'm not old enough and the business is doing well," or even "What would I do then?" Sometimes, it takes an external influence to jumpstart your thinking. It could be a definitive influence, or it may just be a nudge.

Along the way, you are managing your company—often through very different economic cycles and competitive environments. These changing and shifting market conditions can affect all your decisions. To maintain the proper aim on your bullseye, there will be adjustments for these market changes. Predictability and magnitude play a role in this. Some changes you see coming and some you don't. Some changes are subtle, but some could cause seismic shifts in your thinking. I made sure my management team knew to count on one thing being constant: change.

TripTrik—Adjusting When New Information Becomes Available

There are times when your bullseye is very well defined, and you feel you have all the information needed to hit it. It is obvious to you and all those on the journey with you that you are ready to go. The task is now to hit your bullseye. As discussed earlier, the challenge of hitting your bullseye requires planning and marshalling your resources, but it may also require some adjustments along the way. Some can be anticipated; others will be done mid-course as new information becomes available. As your company evolves, the adjustments may take different forms in scale and duration. This is the two-dimensional aspect of aiming. A family car trip—as a child and later as a parent—is a great analogy.

 As a young child, one of five, I remember family vacations always involved a car trip. From our Ohio home, we often drove to Florida and even as far as the Grand Canyon. Back then (1960s and '70s), we would call the American Automobile Association and get a TripTik before we left. This was a little, spiral-bound booklet, about three inches wide and eight inches tall. For a trip to Florida, there might be fifteen pages, each one a map with the interstate or road we were to take in the middle. You started at the top and when you get to the bottom of the page, you turned to the next and started again. The route was always highlighted. This was accompanied by a large conventional fold-out map with the same highlighted route.

We knew where we were going—our bullseye—a specific hotel and the day we were to arrive. The route was also specific; we would always follow it. Sometimes there would be markings of roadwork or an occasional detour but the TripTik always worked. We might glance at the big map before we left, but otherwise we didn't use it. The TripTik was just fine.

For the times, this worked just fine. However, by today's standards, it would almost always be slower and use more gas. Today, when I get in my car at 7 AM on a weekday, my cell phone tells me what route to take to my office and how long it will take. I don't even ask or check it unless it chimes with a pertinent message.

When I take my kids on a vacation by car and need help navigating to a destination, I simply bring up my simple-to-use maps app on my smartphone. I type in where I want to go—my bullseye. The app figures out the best route at that time, displays it, allows me to adjust the view, and automatically reminds me when to turn.

Like map apps, the tools available to businesses today are incredible, allowing us to adjust our aim in real time. Our challenge is to recognize whether we need to adjust our aim or our bullseye.

If your bullseye remains intact and is still relevant after you have begun your journey towards it, don't be afraid or reluctant to adjust your strategy based on new information, intelligence, or analysis. Our ability to gather data, and the speed at which it comes, has increased exponentially. Think of it as a guided missile launch. The bullseye is still the same but shifting winds have altered the path. Your calculation of the path is just as important as the calculation of the bullseye itself. Use the same care and due diligence to plot a new strategy and course when necessary and keep in mind the critical time element with such adjustments.

While TripTiks offered the best information available for the times, our current ability to adjust our business strategies en route is required in order to remain competitive. On even short to medium trips today, almost everyone would expect a computer voice to say that "she" is *recalculating* the route at least once. Business is the same. Focus on your ability to gather relevant information and be prepared to adjust, even if your bullseye stays put. Listen to that voice and keep *recalculating!*

There is an alternative to the need to adjust our aim. This happens when new information leads us to conclude that our bullseye needs to change. Go back to the TripTik. If a hurricane hit our hotel in Florida in the 1960s or '70s while we were traveling, we would not know to stop, turn around, or go to a new destination, at least not until we were well into our journey. Today, we would know it right away and maybe even be able to predict it before we leave. If your bullseye becomes unattainable or the costs to hit it become exorbitant, then clearly a new bullseye needs to be developed or the mission abandoned altogether.

Beware of Noise

In several conversations with business owners who sold their companies, the process that led to the sale struck me as having a lack of intentionality. It was as if something random or at least unrelated happened and a shift occurred in their thinking. This happened to me a few times prior to selling. Here is a good example of a conversation that made me think deeply about more than just the topic at hand.

> I had friends in high school who became stockbrokers—an old term since replaced by "financial advisors" and other clever monikers. They all seemed to be successful and, by the time we were in our mid-thirties, they were living in nice houses, driving nice cars, and playing golf at country clubs. During that time, the stock market had been on a good long run and they had yet to experience a recession or their first big bubble.
>
> I played golf with them occasionally and enjoyed their company, catching up and reminiscing about old times. I always noticed that they would sprinkle in some comments about their work and success too. I chalked it up to our circumstances. They probably assumed since I owned my own business I had money to invest and couldn't help making a pitch for it. It's funny how little they understood about starting your own business and how generally broke you were at the time.
>
> One such friend, Alan, was a little overconfident, telling stories of how well he was doing in the market. Prior to the recession, when the stock market was very high, he became even more enamored with his own performance. After one

golf outing and over beer afterwards, he began talking about his work, quoting percentage returns for the prior years, and how well he had done, beating the market and even Warren Buffett. While I didn't exactly believe it, I couldn't help but ask about a certain stock he bought at a low price. So, I said, "What did you sell it for?" He looked perplexed and said he hadn't sold it yet. I followed up with, "Tell me when you'll you sell it and why?" There were more confused looks, and he said he was holding until something changed. It was peculiar that he didn't have a bullseye and no real estimate or description of what it might be.

The conversation went on to other topics. After we finished another beer and walked to the parking lot, Alan made his last stockbroker services pitch of the day. At this point, I was ready to go but wanted to give him some friendly advice. I hated seeing a friend not thinking things through. I said, "It sounds like you're having a heck of a run; I'm super happy for you. You know some brokers get caught up in thinking how smart they are when they are just confusing brains with a bull market. Don't get caught up in that." I'm not sure it came out as friendly as I wanted, but he got the message.

My only point that day was that buying a stock and watch it go up doesn't demonstrate brains. Selling a stock for a profit greater than the market performed does. Brains are demonstrated by achieving his client's goals including considering things like risk, duration, income needs, taxes, and other considerations along with return. A stock's price in the interim—between buying and selling—is only an indication of value, not a realization of it.

Alan was confusing interim information with hitting the bullseye. Certainly, his clients prescribe a bullseye, or perhaps a target in this case. The target would represent the entire range of satisfactory outcomes; the bullseye would represent their best-case scenario. For example, success might be having a client who was able to retire and having met or exceeded that client's goals for income while maintaining his prescribed base investment. It is not about the price at which he bought a stock or the price it is today.

When I started my business, I was thirty-six years old, with two kids, aged four and six. I didn't think about much other than getting the business up and running. I also had borrowed a huge amount of money; paying off the debt crowded out most other goals.

As my business began to turn profits, and we paid down debt, I began to think about growing the company. We did so throughout the years, both by acquisition and organically. I still did not have many thoughts about selling or realizing the value of my business in other ways but was just operating it as profitably as possible and growing the value of the company. I wasn't doing much long-horizon thinking.

By the time the recession of the late 2000s hit, I was again focused on survival—just as we had in the beginning. We worked hard during this time to become the lowest cost producer possible and benchmarked ourselves as often as possible to make sure we were achieving this bullseye. We went from looking for dollars to quarters to nickels and then even pennies. Every cent counted as the recession dragged on.

As we emerged from this time, several things had changed. Business would not be the same for us or many other companies. It sounded like stories I've heard from the generation that emerged from the Great Depression of the 1930s. Their lives, values, and outlook were forever affected. As for my business, the changes were somewhat subtle but present every day. We began to reconsider the useful lives of assets and, therefore, capital investments more carefully and were reluctant to take some of the same risks we were taking years before. Then, another, more pressing change occurred.

Abrupt Changes

The recession was winding down and the economy had stabilized. While we were not really growing again, it seemed like our business had found its footing and was going to survive intact. Our capital expenditures remained conservative for several years, as we still wanted to see more light coming from the end of the tunnel.

Many of my competitors had not fared as well. Some were sold to other companies and some just shut down, unable to meet cash flow needs. Selling was not on my mind at the time. I was happy to emerge from the recession and was looking forward to more prosperous times. Then, the environment around me changed and new external influences made me reassess what my bullseye should be.

Just as the recession was abating, my former employer, then one of the largest companies in our industry in Ohio, began to experience real problems. They essentially were going broke, even after seven-plus years of growth. They had completed several acquisitions in their (and my) home markets as well as one in Columbus, Ohio, the next nearest major metropolitan market. Their problem was that most, if not all, of these acquisitions had been overpaid. I knew this, since we had bid on many of the same companies.

Overpaying for acquisitions was just the beginning of

their problems. Most of the companies they bought were in trouble themselves. Their assets were old, maintenance neglected for years, and they had little management talent. This was not a surprise; that same management had run these companies to the brink of failure before the acquisition. My former employer had become bloated with debt and lacked the competent management to improve their situation. In the end, their problem was the same as most failing entities. They were ill-managed and ran out of cash.

As the cash crunch hit, banks and major suppliers began to circle. As often happens, the first strike was just one of many before the eventual death blow. Their primary bank forced them into receivership, appointing a trustee to run the company while they searched for a way out of their worsening situation. As this took shape, the only option was to sell the company. They hired a broker and began the process of marketing the company to would-be suitors.

However, the process was short-circuited by a unique set of events. Recessions can make people do strange things. In this case, the owner and his bank made some less-than-optimal decisions and brought in another party—there were now three of them doing things that were out of the ordinary.

In 2010, the company met Steve, a self-made billionaire with a knack for acquiring highly strategic assets at just the right time and, of course, at the right price. He had exited most of his industry holdings a few years earlier and was now primarily a private investor. Believing the bare assets to be worth more at auction than he would have to pay for a going-concern company that size, Steve was clearly interested.

In a creative move a few months later, he purchased the company's debt from their banks for a large discount and had set up a "Stalking Horse" sale arrangement, where a potential buyer signs an agreement to buy a company for a stated price at a future date. Then an auction is conducted to sell the company where the stalking horse can bid but doesn't have to. The company is sold to the highest bidder. There are three possible outcomes. If there are no bids, the stalking horse buys the company for the contract price. If there are bids and the stalking horse is still highest, then the stalking horse buys the company for the new, higher price. Lastly, if there are bids and another company is the highest bidder, the company is sold to this new bidder and the stalking horse is paid a prearranged fee for his trouble.

The twist was that Steve owned the bank debt. That meant he would receive the proceeds of any sale up to the original face amount of the debt, which was over twice as much as he paid. He would win either way, getting the company for a large discount due to buying the bank debt, or getting paid back his purchased debt plus a potentially big profit in less than a year. It was brilliant, but something that could be done only by a well-capitalized buyer. No bank, even a sub-prime lender, would have touched it—a great example of "it takes money to make money." Someone with a lot of cash and an eye for opportunity could do this and profit handsomely. Others need not apply.

It was no surprise that Steve ended up buying my former employer. There were no other bidders, and he would have probably outbid them if there were, at least up to a certain point. So, now I had a new, unfamiliar competitor. His reputation was daunting, as was his wealth—a multi-billionaire in my backyard.

This story helps explain how I began to think about selling my company. It was also a key element in my decision-making process.

My former employer being sold to Steve dramatically affected how I viewed my company, our market, and the future. Not only had the bullseye moved but the entire target was in a new place.

After some Google time and several phone calls to industry people in the know, I got a picture of who Steve was and what he was like as a competitor. I spent months watching and wondering what his end game might be. I came to believe that he would be very aggressive, lowering prices until others left the market and then, with additional market share and influence, raising prices to reap his reward. It was not a strategy for the faint of heart, but he was a big fish in a little pond.

I concluded that I should attempt to join him rather than fight. My plan was rooted in the simple fact that I had a good reputation, was familiar with the market, and that he was based in Las Vegas and not likely to want to run the company himself. After almost six months talking with Steve, trading emails, and meeting in person, I proposed merging our companies with me as CEO of the new combined entity.

Initially, the conversations seemed to be making progress. We seemed to hit it off, both personally and professionally. Steve was easy to talk to and straightforward. He also betrayed very little ego or bravado. If no one had told you, you would have never guessed of his immense success and wealth but also would not have doubted his intelligence.

In the end, we terminated our discussions. The sticking point for me was that I wanted to have autonomy in running the business. The exception I offered, since he would be majority owner, was that he could fire me but that would trigger a "put" option on my ownership shares. In other words, I would have had an option to force the purchase of my shares at a predetermined price or formula. It protected me from being forced out of my company without being paid market price or even a slight premium. For Steve, the sticking point was a lack of control since he, as majority owner, would be acting as the new company's bank.

We both appreciated and respected each other's position and truly believed we both wanted to proceed. The sticking points were just too sticky for both of us. So, we parted ways amicably. To this day, I know I could call Steve on his cell and we would have a good conversation.

However good I felt about my dealings with Steve and how they ended, I knew I now had to deal with him as a competitor. I knew he was probably as big a threat as my business had ever seen.

After we called it quits with our merger discussions, I began to consider my options. His strategy to dominate the market was being put in place. Prices were dropping and our margins were squeezed. I was confident we were the lowest cost operator in our market but that would not matter if his "investment" was to include market share increases purchased via low prices to all our customers. Potentially, this meant we would earn lower and lower returns until our business was unable to continue.

I also knew we had some time. This would not happen overnight, and we had built a loyal customer base. It wasn't impenetrable but it would hold the barbarians at the gate for several years at a minimum. This led me to pursue a sale of my company. We had several good (but not great) years to show and the economy was gaining strength. I called a well-respected broker and began discussions. Within a few months, we were contacting prospective buyers and having conversations about possible deals.

The process took about nine months and, in the end, we did not receive a proposal I considered sufficient, meaning a combination of what I thought was reasonable versus what I thought were the risks of continuing. The additional nine months of running my business had also eased some of my concerns. While Steve had hired people to run his new business, they were not terribly good. For the most part, they seemed to be running it like their Los Angeles business—and LA is not Ohio by a long shot. They seemed to stumble at every turn and were not getting the attention they needed from Steve or his senior management. (Years later, Steve said he had not even been in Ohio after he bought the company.)

I was disappointed in not selling my company but resolute and confident (at least outwardly) that I had made the right decision. We buckled down and worked as hard as ever to protect what we had grown. We lost some ground in the market but generally only the ground that we consciously gave up. It became a game of appeasement and survival. It reminded me of once being told "be careful not to aggravate the bear"—meaning competing with a dominant company in your market. You can be careful and live off scraps, and occasionally get a good meal, but always remember that the bear can take you out with one swipe of his powerful paw.

We continued for several years and then the "competitor gods" sent us a gift. Steve abruptly sold his company to the next largest existing competitor in our market. While this created a very large business in our home market, it also meant one less competitor. In these cases, companies like mine can generally benefit as much or more than the acquirer. When a large competitor leaves the market, the benefits include picking up market share (the acquirer rarely keeps all the seller's business) and increased margins.

The market did improve, and we began experiencing increases in sales and margins. It also changed my outlook and moved my target—again. There is a balance between being reactive to changes in the business environment and being patient enough to understand trends. We were adjusting quickly but not haphazardly. However, these were seismic shifts in our market that warranted a change in our bullseye and aim. Being opportunistic can sound bad but it is the crux of solid strategic decisions. Opportunities are to be taken advantage of and they do not remain available indefinitely.

We began to reinvest in our equipment and people at a faster rate. It was not breakneck nor beyond our financial means but at a quicker pace. I also began to explore potential acquisitions and greenfield plant sites. I knew we had a window to make some moves but couldn't tell how long the window would be open. We just proceeded at determined pace.

For about three years, our good fortune continued. We had three record profit years in a row and were making net and gross margins that put us among the very best in our entire industry. I was thrilled, but the recession had instilled in me what I had heard about the generation from the Great Depression. I never took for granted how well things were going and remained conservative while pursuing new opportunities. Or as Intel CEO Andy Grove[3] might put it: I remained paranoid.

Despite having decided against selling for now, the possibility of selling remained in my conscious thoughts. It tempered my thinking more often and made me aware that the value of my

---

3   Grove, Andrew. *Only the Paranoid Survive: How to Identify and Exploit the Crisis Points that Challenge Every Business*. London: Profile Books, 1996.

company was ever changing, both because of its profitability and the environment we operated in. I did not set any timetable for an eventual sale, but I now used it as a benchmark of sorts for many long-term and strategic decisions.

CHAPTER 12

THE SENSIBILITY OF SELLING MY COMPANY

"Congratulations! Way to go! I'm so happy for you!" These are the words that you often hear after a great accomplishment or milestone, whether you graduated from school, got married, or had a child. In business, it's the same. You get congratulated for starting a business, making your first sale, or landing a big contract. It can be exhilarating and rewarding, but in business, as in life, the most meaningful compliments are usually at the end of a long journey. (Plus, I don't want to be jinxed along the way.)

On a personal level (and in a funny way), wouldn't it be more appropriate to congratulate someone *after* they got a job and succeeded in it, instead of at graduation? Would they be more appropriate *after* a long marriage, celebrating a fiftieth anniversary? Better *after* a child has grown up and is happily married, with a rewarding career?

On a professional level, this is even more true. The best I ever felt receiving congratulations was when I sold my business. It was one of many other significant milestones along the way but was truly the capstone of a professional career. It was, in many ways, the only real goal that I always strived for—creating value in my business and then realizing it. The *creating* part is ongoing and can have its ups and downs. The *realizing* part is the pinnacle. It's when you realize the existing value that there is a confirmed reason to celebrate. Otherwise, you are just happy, maybe rightfully so, but you are only leading the game at halftime. I'll return to this idea, but a slightly off-track example might be helpful.

At the end of our third record year in a row, just before I sold, a similar-size competitor came up for sale. The owners were of retirement age and wanted out. While it was a stretch for us, we went after the business because of the close fit with our footprint in the market. We had very little overlap and many complementary elements. It seemed we were the leading bidder as we approached the time to proceed with a legal agreement. I was about to declare victory when I received confirmation that another buyer had stepped up their bid, offering 15 percent more than my last proposal. I was already at my top bid, so it took little time to decide we would not increase our offer.

The winning bid was hard to figure out. I knew the company for sale almost as well as my own. I doubted there was another business with the same synergies as ours. The winner was a company from outside of our market, a newcomer to our part of the world. They had a reputation for being an aggressive acquirer and had grown quickly in recent years. As things died down and the deal closed, I received a phone call from Lee, the newcomer's owner.

I had known him, only casually, for a very short time but he immediately made an offer for my business after our first in-person meeting. This was after only four hours of time together and without even looking at our books. I couldn't tell if his offer was in earnest or just a "throw it on the wall and see if it sticks" attempt. Either way, it was a more than reasonable offer. In fact, it was about twice what we were offered a few years before. I think I'm a fairly good poker player and tried to slow down the discussions. I could tell he was eager but also seemed a bit anxious for an answer. He wanted to proceed immediately or go on to his next acquisition target.

I also wasn't confident about what others in the market might pay for my company. While Lee's offer seemed very good, I didn't have the information that would make me sure of the value of my business. So, I decided to hire Phil, an investment banker, to act as my business broker. He was respected and highly regarded in our industry. He also knew Lee and had facilitated a business sale to him a few years earlier. My bet, so to speak, was that Phil would bring in more than his fees in price and/or value. Price is straightforward. Value included dealing with negotiations and getting the terms and conditions right. Some of that value you can put a number on and some you can't.

Before I formally hired Phil, we had several discussions regarding potential buyers. Frankly, Phil was doing a good job of staying in touch with me and continuing to show that he could add value. It was a big part of why I eventually chose him. He understood my business and how to maximize its value. He could also identify interested buyers.

During this time, I was learning from him and doing some soul-searching myself. My company was like my baby. I had poured a lot of myself into it and money was not the biggest part. I had worked for years starting, building, growing, and finetuning it into a world-class business. I had put my whole heart and soul into it for seventeen years, never spending a day *not* thinking about it.

My heart lobbied hard to continue but my head was in charge of this committee. I knew it was not fiscally responsible to have all my eggs in one basket. Throughout the ownership of my business, it had always made up over 90 percent of my net worth. While the business was still growing and profitable, if I continued to own and operate it, the lack of diversification in my net worth would not change anytime soon. It was obviously a risk.

On an intellectual level, it would be a mistake to pass on Lee's offer. It would be one thing if I could have taken money out of the business and invested it elsewhere, thereby diversifying my personal assets. However, this was not realistic as the business needed most of the capital it generated to continue to replace assets and upgrade our facilities. I could have cut back on this, but it would have risked the value created by almost two decades of hard work. Also, growing businesses always attract better offers than stagnant ones do.

I could have taken on partners or talked to private equity investors. However, as I recounted earlier, my experience with partners was not so good. I did not want to risk another bad episode in dealing with one. Private equity seemed like a good option on its face. It can offer an opportunity to sell part of the company thereby taking some capital off the table and diversifying my net worth. However, I also decided against this option for a simple reason: control. Private equity firms buy into companies with an exit strategy in mind from the beginning. They want to know when they will be able to get out and they want to control that aspect. I did not mind the "get out" part, but the "control" part was out of the question. I had absolutely crossed the line into where control and autonomy were coveted parts of my life. I was unwilling to give that up. It was a luxury that had turned into a necessity.

I returned to the issue of having 90 percent of my net worth tied up in a single asset, my company. Despite my personal and emotional ties to my business, I saw the reality of risk in not diversifying my net worth. It was as if you retired and had all your savings with a stock brokerage house. What you would think of a broker recommending investing 90 percent of your nest egg in the stock of a single company? You would think him insane and take your money elsewhere. It was the same for me and my business.

Tipping Point

The final piece of logic that made my decision to sell easier was timing. I had started my business in 2000 and had experienced some minor swings in the economy. In fact, dating back to my start in the industry, I had only experienced a few downturns which were generally short in duration. All were unpleasant but bearable and we survived without dramatic cuts or losses. However, one major swing, the recession starting in the late 2000s, was a doozy. There were years of miserable business and not knowing if we would make it. There were also businesses going broke and many others losing much of their value. My concern with not selling was that I would risk owning and running the business into the next correction, or worse, recession. Then I might have to sell for reasons outside my control. I was fifty-four, and the thought of needing money for a health or family issue, or just wanting to retire, would be a possibility in the next ten years or so. Being forced to sell the business when it is weathering a recession would be a disaster. Besides, you are supposed to "sell high" in the stock market so why not with your business—especially when that business is your biggest asset.

More and more, I began to think of my business this way—as an asset I should carefully consider the best time to sell. If you thought your shares of Apple were the at the highest they would be for the next ten years, even including inflation and the time-value of money, wouldn't you sell them now? As I looked at my situation, I concluded it was that time. We had just recorded the highest profit year ever and judging by the multiples being paid for other businesses in our industry, we were as close to top valuation as I had seen or could imagine. I also knew that once people see the top, money for acquisitions dries up. In our industry, once the three-year forecasts have a negative number in the third year, it is over. The acquisition spigot all but turns off and valuations and multiples fall. For me and my family, I wasn't willing to take the risk.

My conversations with Phil took on more specifics. He asked if a certain company would make sense as an acquirer, or if I knew the CEO. Could he approach different firms and just present my company, without any identifying information, as a possible seller? I let him proceed, and some of these conversations led to interest and meetings, eventually with potential buyers who indicated my company's value was similar to, albeit lower than, Lee's offer.

After several meetings with these potential buyers, Phil convinced me to let him re-engage with Lee, the owner of the company that just bought into our market. He felt that Lee would want to proceed quickly and would lose interest if we slowed down and pitted him against others. Essentially, the meetings we had with others were a confirmation of interest and of Phil's estimated value for my business. Lee looked to have the highest valuation, and Phil was confident that now was time to re-engage him and push for an agreement.

It was interesting to see how my mindset and outlook had evolved. Events and trends in the market had not changed. No internal elements had shifted. It was a transformation in *me* and how I looked more intently at owning my business. It was rooted in the first time I considered selling and my present thinking about my business's value and marketability. On my own, I had decided to aim at a different bullseye. Until now, however, this had been without specific timing.

Lee's offer was on the very high side of a relevant multiple of EBITDA for our business. The EBITDA figure he was using was from our most recent year, a record high. I knew it was a great offer and maybe the best offer I could get for many years. He was just the right guy at the right time. With Phil pushing to re-engage Lee, I told him to run with it.

Hiring Phil paid off almost immediately, resulting in a Letter of Intent (LOI) from Lee, outlining the price and general terms and conditions of a sale. While not binding, an LOI does state the most important aspects of a deal and serves as a framework for attorneys to draft the legal agreements. With Phil's input, we agreed to a LOI within two weeks (with significant earnest money) and then turned it over to the attorneys.

As the buyer, Lee's attorneys took on the responsibility to draft the agreements. I met with my attorney and went through the LOI and we waited. It was about a month before we saw the first draft and could start responding with comments and proposed changes. It is not unusual to have a lot of changes, but most were just factual corrections rather than significant or material changes.

I knew that I had to prepare myself and have the right mindset going into this sale. This meant knowing what I would accept and, most importantly, when I would walk away. It was about having a clear and well-defined bullseye in mind. When negotiating anything, especially the sale of your business, you need to have clearly in your mind the lines you will not cross. This not only makes things easier but protects you against yourself and human nature. Without such care and discipline, we all can make bad decisions in the heat of the battle.

I reminded myself of the time spent owning a car dealership. Then, my general manager and I would go to auto auctions, held once or twice a week, and buy used cars to take back to our lot and sell. A day or two before the auction, we would review the list of cars to be auctioned and decide the maximum we would bid on each. On the day of the auction, we would arrive and inspect the cars to verify condition and adjust our "max" numbers.

When I first attended these auctions, the general manager would occasionally bid over our agreed maximum number on a car. When I questioned him, he usually stated that it was extra clean or in better condition that we anticipated. What I eventually saw was that he was susceptible to doing things that were not logical while in the middle of bidding. The heat of the battle can cause the same reaction in almost everyone. To buy a certain car, while standing with others wanting the same thing, and in all the noise and commotion of an auction, he would let the circumstances get the better of him.

My experience with these auctions taught me the importance of knowing your limits and sticking to them no matter what the noise and commotion was doing to you. Throughout my business career, it often kept me from over-paying, overpromising, underbidding, and other business sins. Selling my business to Lee would be no different. I had to understand those limits and be willing to approach them but not go beyond.

Lee's team was reasonable on most issues; we rarely had sticking points as we negotiated the legal agreements. The process seemed to be going very well. Even as smooth as things appeared to be, I braced myself for the one or two issues that seem to come up and jeopardize any closing. It was just inevitable; it had happened to me often in the past.

A few weeks before scheduled closing, the first one occurred. As I was attempting to arrange lease assign-ments for some of the properties that our plants sat on, one company became a problem. It was a very large, publicly traded company and generally very professional, but they had a regional manager who saw himself as much smarter and much more important than he was. (I had dealt with him for years and knew him well: a typical mid-level manager of a large company with a Napoleonic personality.)

We met at a local restaurant to go over the lease assignment. He immediately began giving me his typical, omni-important, self-serving line of ego-driven B.S. Eventu-ally, he said he wasn't going to approve the assignment and he would have to think about what *he* wanted to do. There was no reasoning, no factual basis, no legal basis, nothing that made sense. He made it abundantly clear that he would control what I did, including who I sold my company to.

I was surprised but not completely shocked. A few years earlier, I had caught him in violation of a federal anti-trust law on pricing. It was a somewhat minor issue for him but one that affected my company greatly. When confronted, he first denied the facts, then denied the legality of my argument, but eventually made the appropriate price adjustments—but without admitting to any wrongdoing, not even a whiff.

So, I was prepared for him. I asked point blank if he intended to assign the lease so we could close in time. He said no, so I got up and said I was leaving and had to make some calls. As I walked to my car, I replayed the conversation in my head, still reeling from his pompous statements. When I got in my car, I looked at my cell phone and felt better. It had been sitting innocently on the table in the restaurant and recorded everything he said. I knew I had leverage. His statements, legally recorded, constituted Tortious Interference—every bit as bad as the anti-trust violation. The only thing to appreciate about the guy was his consistency (and maybe his cluelessness). He was always willing to break the law.

I replayed the conversation a few times and then made calls to my attorney and to a senior management member of the company he worked for. I told them both the same thing. Here was the conversation we had, and I believe that this guy is trying to intentionally interfere with my business and cause harm. At the very least, his actions, if unchecked, would cause a very ugly and expensive lawsuit.

After a series of follow-up calls and complaints, the issue was resolved. We got the assignment done and could close on time. One crisis averted.

My preparation for this guy's interference, whether he knew it was illegal or not, was the key to handling it in the most expeditious way possible. Recording the conversation may seem underhanded, but it was appropriate (and legal) given his history and probably helped underscore the seriousness of the matter. Whatever was passed along to the large company's officers made the roadblock go away.

Just a day before closing, the next jeopardizing issue came up. One of the properties I owned was where a key plant was located. In a title search, a public filing turned up that raised the possibility of a claim on the property. At worst, it could mean that we did not have clear title to the property. My attorney felt it was not legitimate and a non-issue, but Lee's attorneys felt otherwise. The back-and-forth had continued for weeks and so there was still an outstanding, unresolved issue—on the day before closing.

Crossing the Finish Line

My attorney informed me that they wanted a bond or guarantee in an amount equal to twice the value of the property and to hold me responsible for damages if a claim was made. I did not agree to this. It was too much risk, almost unlimited risk, and for an unlimited amount of time. I discussed it with my attorney, who felt that the other attorneys were driving it harder than Lee and his management team were. I knew this was the defining issue still left and I had two choices: tell them no and watch the deal blow up or find a way to salvage the deal with a palatable offer to resolve their concern.

Fortunately, Lee's son was in my conference room nearby, writing some emails and doing miscellaneous work. I thought some about what was reasonable and what I could accept and then made my way down to the conference room. It was about 3 PM.

I had been welcoming and cheerful to Lee and his son throughout the entire process. Everything had gone smoothly, and both were professional and friendly. Now, I got to test their resolve while still wanting to close. I walked into the conference room and asked the son if he had a few minutes to talk. I explained the call with my attorney and my surprise that his attorneys were taking such a firm stand on this property issue. The conversation was very matter of fact and he stood his ground. I didn't see him wanting to move on the issue.

I had to do something to make progress, so I pivoted to a more confrontational attitude. I explained the legal basis for why this was not an issue and that he should close without a bond or guarantee. I went further. As an option, I would keep the property and rent it to him. He said no to both and that he wanted the property. Then I said I would buy him a similar property nearby that was for sale and move the plant there for him. He said no again and reiterated that he wanted this property. I knew it wasn't logical and he was trying to get his bond/guarantee. So, now I began to use a little profanity and raised my voice somewhat—not yelling or screaming but making sure he knew I was about to walk out. It was then he offered a much lower bond amount and capped the amount of time for possible claims, I told him it was a non-starter and took a few steps to the door. I turned back and told him that he may as well fly back home because the closing wasn't happening tomorrow if at all.

He said, "Wait, let me think about this. Maybe there is something that makes sense we both could agree to." I stood waiting and, after what seemed like an hour (probably thirty seconds), he proposed a much better offer. I told him I'd think about it even though it was below my threshold and now at an acceptable level. I did that because I was still a bit concerned that there might be other nagging issues that were not brought up yet. I wanted a little "dry powder" if I needed it between then and the closing on the next day. I walked the rest of the way to the door, turned and said, "I hope we are done with issues brought up at the last minute." He said there was one other. We went over that issue, worth less than 0.03 percent of the total deal. He needed a win, so I told him that was fine and that he could deduct it from the price. Then he talked about "a few other smaller things" he wanted to discuss. I opened the door to the conference room and stated very succinctly how I felt about this going on and on. I said, "I'll tell you what. Take all the items that add up to $10,000 or less and put them on a list and take them off the price. I'm done with last minute negotiating of things that should have been brought up weeks ago." With that, I turned to walk out, and as I did, he asked if I was going to be on the conference call set up by the attorneys that started in five minutes. I said "nope" and walked away.

I walked up to my office and sat down at my desk. I thought overall it went very well. I had got them to back off the big issue, let them win a small issue, and hopefully stopped further last-minute negotiations. I then realized that the impression I made on walking out needed to remain intact, so I grabbed some paperwork and headed out the door. It was the equivalent of a good stage exit.

I was home for a few hours when Phil called and left a message. He said that Lee had called him several times and was worried I would not close. I didn't call back right away but got a few text messages from him later in the evening. Finally, I called him back. He said Lee was still calling him and sounded more worried every call. I was not a masochist, but I did want the impression to stick that I was done negotiating. A lot of people won't stop negotiating until they get some sort of sign that the other side was truly done or ready to walk away. Even though that was not exactly the case, I wanted them to have that impression. I let him know he could let Lee off the hook, and we'd close tomorrow. It was about 9 PM.

The next morning, I went into the office and found Lee's son. He asked me if we are still on schedule to close that day. I told him we were, and generally returned to a warmer, friendly appearance. We closed that day with no more hitches.

While no one wants to think of negotiating as a game, to some degree it is. It's about keeping your sights on the bullseye, adjusting aim, and waiting and watching to see if the target has been moved without advance notice. Adjustments and trade-offs are always made, but it was important for me to keep limits in mind and not get caught up in getting to the finish line without consideration of how I get there. I am sure Lee, his son, and others played their side of the game as well. In the end, we both got what we wanted. I got a very good price for my company and away from the concentration of my net worth in one asset, and Lee got a very good company with great people.

CHAPTER 13

SOME OF THE BEST BUSINESS LESSONS I EVER LEARNED

We've all been influenced by a few words spoken at a timely moment. Sometimes it comes from a trusted source and sometimes it comes unexpectedly. I have carried around a number of these for years and they still guide me today.

I have often found that these turns of phrase make sense on their own, but they almost always come from somebody that embodies them. They live these words every day. They show them in their actions; it's part of their value system.

Many are from people some would call mentors. I don't think I ever had a "mentor" in the traditional sense of the word, but I've had indispensable advice given to me over my career. To receive and embrace advice from a trusted source is quite a gift. Here are a few of my favorites.

Jack—"Work Hard"

Before I was sixteen, I worked for a company owned by a friend of my dad. In a rented shop next door, a man named Jack had started his own plumbing business, and by then had many trucks and plumbers working for him. I used to go into his office and buy snacks from his vending machines a few times a week. He was always at the front counter, with all the plumbing supplies behind him, and was friendly from the first time we met.

> Jack would always ask how I was and what I was doing when I visited. I'd hang around and talk for a few minutes, enjoying the company of an adult who seemed interested in anything I was doing or had to say. One day, as I got my snack and was ready to leave, Jack said, "Hey Jim, I've noticed something." When I asked what that was, he told me he comes to work every day early and gets his crews started, and he noticed that I was always the first one in at the business next door. He said, "I've noticed that for the last three years and I've noticed that you always work hard all day. You know that's a good thing."
>
> I still thought this was a casual conversation but appreciated the compliment. He kept talking. "Jim, if there is one thing I've learned about being successful, it's that you have to work hard. You can be smart, and you can be lucky, but you have to work hard. You've got that. Just make sure you remember it."

I've thought about that simple advice often and given it many times, of course mostly to my kids. Over the years, I knew it also meant to care about your work and go about it diligently. It meant to not go about work haphazardly or disregard effort. It meant if you are going to go about life, there is no replacement for good, honest, hard work.

Roger—"Get Your Degree"

At the same business I worked at, next to Jack's, was where I made lifelong friends and would periodically visit in the years after high school. They were older than me but had always treated me as a peer. My visits were somewhat sporadic, but I always looked forward to catching up with them.

After half of my freshman year in college, I quit school. My grades had been good, but I just didn't feel like school mattered. I was in that "I am smarter than most people already" phase that some of us get into. I was dabbling in different jobs and investigating getting into business myself. None of this had a future but I didn't know that at the time.

About three months after I quit school, I stopped into the office next to Jack's to see everyone. Roger, sales manager for the company, was sitting at this desk. We chatted for a bit and Roger told me a few jokes, as he usually did. I meandered through the rest of the office and said my hellos and chatted with everyone. It was a fun break but eventually I headed for the door. As I reached the door, Roger, the only one left in the room, asked me what I had planned. He knew I had quit college. I gave him whatever my standard answer was at the time, which amounted to almost nothing logical.

He looked at me and said, "You know something, that sounds promising, but I'm not sure you are going to be happy." I'm sure I looked puzzled and so he continued. He told me about his good friend, Phil, who owned the company. They had just been bought out by a large international firm, and now he attended meetings in New York and Switzerland as part of his duties. He told me of one meeting that he was at with Phil. "We all went to this big meeting in New York. The new Swiss owners were there. Before the meeting starts, everyone is milling around and introducing themselves. At that level, it's funny how all these successful executives from all over the world usually end up talking about what college degree they got and where they went to school. You know, I went here and got this and then I went here and got that."

Then he told me something I didn't know. He said that Phil, someone as gregarious and friendly as anyone else, looked like a fish out of water. No one was talking to him and he looked like he was ignoring everyone in return. Roger said, "Phil introduced himself to others, but when the subject of college came up, Phil had to admit he never went. He was embarrassed. He didn't need to be because you and I know that Phil is smart as hell, but he was embarrassed, and it showed."

Roger let me know the point wasn't about whether Phil or I were smart but people's perception about a college degree. It was an important part of who we are, especially at a certain level of business. It was a club they were all in—all but Phil. He went on to say that while he wasn't the best student, his master's degree in chemistry conveyed something to others. He spoke succinctly, in his slight West Virginia accent, saying, "It wasn't that I was a chemistry wiz. It's just that they knew I had accomplished something academically. I had made it through that, and I was just like them." He finished with, "Think about going back and getting your degree. Show everyone that you can. It may not make a damn difference in how smart you are, but it makes you part of the club, and where you are going, you are going to want to be part of the club."

Roger's argument was more about accomplishment, perseverance, and my potential. I think he foresaw that I had potential to be successful in business and that the degrees would make a difference—maybe to a banker or customer someday, or maybe just to me. Later in life, I translated this into something broader. It was about knowledge, experience, and accomplishments for me and about certifications, credentialing, and qualifications for my company. These always gave us a step up on our competition and put us closer to our goals.

Steve—"Make Sure You're Always Right"

After taking Roger's advice and deciding I was going back to college, I transferred to a school near my hometown. I also needed to pay for school, so I enrolled in night classes and looked for a job. I found a job at a construction materials company run by someone I had known, barely, in high school. Steve was four years older than me but, since he was married to my cousin, we each knew the other. I met him again on my first day at work.

As the operations manager, Steve took a little time to talk to me that first day but then sent me off to a plant to start work as a quality control technician. In the first few weeks, we would see each other and talk a bit but not about anything in depth. I worked hard and tried to learn everything I could about my new job and industry. I wanted to make a difference, even if it was just a "college job." Over time, he must have taken notice and would talk to me more often, eventually giving me some miscellaneous projects to work on. After nine months, I began to spend more and more time with him in the main office, doing whatever he needed help on.

After a year and a half, I had earned enough of his trust to assist with projects of increasing importance to the business. I was the first person to put the company's annual budget in a spreadsheet program (Lotus 1-2-3 for history buffs). Prior to that, it was always done by hand, in pencil and greenline paper, with the columns added up by hand with a desk calculator. While I didn't have line authority, I was gaining influence, and the work became more fun and rewarding.

One day, Steve asked me to sit in a meeting with our largest supplier. The meeting was to cover information on different types of materials and pricing. Steve had given me the background information to study, and I had looked it over beforehand. When the day of the meeting came, I did not have any formal role and wasn't expected to say anything, so I sat in the room and listened.

I watched Steve go through information with the suppliers. Over the course of an hour, he had covered all the possible combinations of materials, logistics, and pricing. He was leading the discussion and clearly knew more about this company's products than their own people. He concluded by asking for a price reduction based on his analysis. The supplier representatives were good guys, but it was clear they had not studied their own material enough to know what Steve did. I watched as they asked questions and fumbled through logic they did not fully understand. Eventually, they agreed to review his materials and get back to us. A few days later, they agreed to Steve's request for new pricing.

Months later, Steve announced he was leaving the company for a new job. He and I talked a lot before he left. He felt I could take on greater responsibility and encouraged me to reach for it. As one of these conversations turned to specifics, he offered some simple advice. He said, "You remember the meeting we had with that supplier a few months ago?" I nodded yes, so he continued, "When you are going to be in a meeting like that, or any situation like that, whether with a supplier or customer or the boss, make sure you know more than anyone else in the room, make sure you're always right." He ended with emphasis on that past part. It wasn't the most elegant way of saying it, but the concept hit home.

His advice wasn't about being right as much as it was about being prepared. Know the facts. Be able to recite them back and forth, and slice and dice all the data in every way possible. Steve was often the smartest guy in the room. He could sometimes come off as arrogant, but it was always about the facts and being prepared. He knew it was hard to beat the facts and preparation. It's good to be right.

As an aside, I also knew Steve never meant this literally for every situation. He demonstrated that always being "right" with customers and employees wasn't the key. It often was important, but he never confused it with inappropriate or demeaning behavior towards others. It could be a fine line, but he knew the difference.

Paul—"Look Up When You Are Talking to Someone"

After Steve left for his new job, I worked hard to take his place, and in a short time was named general manager. I was only twenty-three years old and felt a big surge in my self-worth. I had graduated with my bachelor's degree and went right into the MBA program. Every day, I worked hard to prove myself worthy of the title of general manager.

Along with my new duties, I was getting involved in our accounting department. The company president wasn't much of a numbers guy and seemed happy to let me dig into it. We had a competent accounting manager but lacked anyone with skills above him. There was no controller or CFO, so I soon saw a void that needed to be filled.

One of my MBA courses at the time was Management Accounting. It was a typical advanced-level accounting course and was taught by Paul, the retired CFO of a very large regional lumber company. His classes were always fun and made you think—always a sign of a good accounting professor. One night in class, he mentioned some of his work as a "part-time" CFO. He would spend a day or two a week helping companies that didn't have a CFO or didn't need a full-time one. It started me thinking of my own company's predicament.

After the semester ended, I approached Paul and asked if he would consider a similar, part-time position with the company I worked for. We talked for a bit and, after a meeting where I explained our need for help and guidance, he agreed to come to work for us as a part-time consultant.

I was pleased and relieved to have him aboard. Together we made a list of priorities for him to work on, consisting mostly of helping upgrade our systems and our people. He was great at systems and organization and seemed to have processes and procedures for everything.

Over the following months, Paul would be in the office a day or two a week and usually stop in my office to give updates on his various initiatives. I was interested in what he was doing but not terribly concerned. I had confidence in his ability and was sure he would accomplish what we had set out for him to work on. Besides, I had other more pressing things going on in operations. We were moving plants and installing a new customer service center and my plate was full.

One day Paul came to the open door of my office and knocked. He asked if he could come in and talk about a few things. That's just the way Paul was: a super-successful, retired, seventy-year-old CFO of a big lumber company asking the twenty-three-year-old hotshot general manager if he might have a few minutes. I looked up and said, "Sure," and went back to working on my computer. He sat down and started to go over his list, but I remained focused on what I was doing. I was listening and felt I could easily do both. I'd look up once in a while and acknowledge his comments or agree to whatever he was talking about, as needed.

Paul finished and said thanks and smiled like he always did. I smiled back and thanked him for the update. That was when he is supposed to get up and leave my office, but instead, he stayed put. I looked up again and he said, "Can I tell you a story?" I didn't feel I had time for a story about credit and collections or whatever there was left to talk about, but I was polite and said "sure." Paul started: "When

I was at the lumber company, I worked for the grandson of the founder and then CEO. He was a very busy guy with the business and a lot of other family matters. I never saw him not working, and he was always the first person in the office and last out. Despite all that, every time any person walked in to see him, no matter if it was me or a secretary or the janitor, Pete would put down whatever he was doing, lean across his desk, and focus on the person in front of him. You could tell he genuinely cared what they were saying. Or even if he didn't, he still conveyed that he cared about what they had to say just as much as the person talking did. He knew if it was important to them then it had to be important to him."

I went flush. I knew who he was talking about: me. I stared at my computer for a few seconds, not knowing what to say. Finally, I turned the monitor away from me and looked at Paul. He was still smiling but giving me a knowing look. I swallowed and said, "I'm sorry, Paul. I didn't mean to be disrespectful to you." Paul smiled a bit more and responded, "Jim, it's not about me. I know you are busy and busy with important things for this company. I just want you to know for the sake of the people that work for you. It means a lot if they know you care. No matter what they have to say, they want to know the boss values them and their time," he paused, "enough to look up and listen like you care."

At the time, it was a lesson contributing to my maturity, but as time went by, I looked at it as more than that. It was a lesson on valuing another's time and thoughts. I was used to "doing" a lot, managing and juggling many things and multiple people at one time. I felt I had the capacity to manage this way, but it was a misguided belief that because I *could* multi-task that I *should* multi-task—and do so all the time. It was a lesson I remind myself of often. Look up and meet the eyes of whomever gives you their time and thoughts. It's of value.

John Pepper—"No More Meetings Where Nothing Gets Decided and Nothing Gets Done"

Through my philanthropic work, I've had the chance to meet many fascinating and successful people. I have been constantly amazed at how the passion and dedication that made them so successful at work fully transfers to issues in philanthropy they feel are important. John Pepper is one such example. He is the former CEO of Procter & Gamble and a legend among business CEOs of the last several decades. I had the good fortune to meet John when we were both working on issues for at-risk families with young children.

Over the years, John and I have been together in many meetings, and I even get to say that he served on the board of trustees of an organization while I was Chairman. It continues to be an honor and pleasure to work with him on issues that we both care deeply about.

A few years ago, when I was Chair of this organization and John was on the board, he and I would see each other every couple of weeks in a meeting or for breakfast or talk on the phone. I respect John tremendously and always try and respect his time. One morning, we had a meeting with several other board members and senior staff at this organization. As Chair, I co-led this meeting with the Executive

Director (ED) of the organization.

As the meeting got started, the ED and I laid out the objective and the conversation started. Unfortunately, as can often happen in meetings with a diverse group of volunteer board members for a non-profit, the conversation meandered and even took a few off-topic tangents. Both the ED and I steered the conversation as best we could but were not assertive enough. Soon, an hour had past and the meeting was over and we really had not accomplished much. There were some courses of action to explore, but the meeting and outcome were not very effective. I knew this and was frustrated but had also come to expect this type of meeting to happen at times.

As we filed out of the conference room, John slowed to walk side-by-side with me. He edged closer and clearly wanted to chat quietly, out of earshot of the others. Then he spoke. "You know, Jim, I'm willing to do anything for this organization and will show up for meetings when you need me." He paused and looked me in the eye. "But I don't need to attend any more meetings where nothing gets decided and nothing gets done." Ouch. I nodded my head and agreed.

John was not coarse about it, but maybe a little frustrated—as I was. He was making the simple point that everyone's time needs to be valued and respected. A few days later I repeated the conversation to the ED and talked about it. I knew we needed to be more considerate of everyone's time and particularly people like John Pepper. He no doubt had endless opportunities on how to spend his time and with which organizations. We needed to appropriately value that and make sure that when we called him for a meeting or for advice, that the conversation is well laid out, effective, and efficient.

I also think John was making a general point about such meetings and discussions. He didn't say it at the time, but I knew he was urging me to take better care of setting an agenda and sticking to it. He was telling me to be a better leader albeit in a nice way. His comments made me realize my responsibility in such settings include guarding valuable time. I was lucky to have him (and many others) as an asset on our board and to be able to tap into his vast knowledge and expertise. I needed to be careful not to abuse this privilege.

John's comments that day have stuck with me. Since then, I have guarded my own time better and found that my focus and enthusiasm is better when I do get involved in such matters. Of course, you can't always predict when and where you will get drawn into spending unproductive time, but you can learn from the past and avoid many such timewasters and thus improve your own time management. I can also repeat John's quote to others as I have now been known to do.

Paul—"It Takes the Same Time to Do It Early"

The same Paul who came to help our company as a part-time CFO had another lasting lesson he imparted to me. He was the classic CFO of a successful medium-sized company. He knew how to do every job in accounting and administration firsthand and do it well. Without looking at a calendar or notice in the mail, he knew what reports and forms were due and when. He had been with us for a couple of months when he wandered into my office.

"Jim, do you have a minute?" He was always polite and considerate, even when people didn't deserve it. I was my normal busy self but knew Paul would have something he thought was important to share. He said, "I got a notice that we were late filing a payroll tax return. Take a look." I looked it over, a computer-generated letter from the IRS. It said we were late paying some tax for the last quarter and owed a small fine and a little bit of interest. I looked up and said, "Well, at least it's only $100 or so. I guess it could have been worse. Did you talk to Don about it?" He said he had and would keep an eye on future returns, but something was still nagging at him. I prodded him a bit to tell me more. He said, "I've been going back over the tax filings of the past few years and this isn't new. The company has been late filing something at least ten times, and I haven't looked at all the reports yet."

I knew Don, our Accounting Manager, had been swamped with work for some time and figured this kind of stuff was going on but didn't pay a lot of attention to it, as the dollars were somewhat minor, usually $50-200. I always said something to him, when I saw the notices, but he always had an excuse so I never pushed it beyond a light admonition. Paul said he noticed the same thing. He said, "Don gets it, but he just doesn't change. I said something to him when I first started here. He acknowledged the importance of timely filings, but he's just one of those people who is always a little late. You know it. He is always a little late coming to work, a little late to meetings, and a little late on these filings."

I asked Paul what he thought we should do. I knew he had something in mind before he walked in my office. Paul said, "Let's call Don in here, in front of you, and talk to him. I'll handle it, but I want you in the room and your words of support." So, I called Don and he came down the hall into my office. Paul was incredibly kind but firm at the same time. He made something clear that even I wasn't thinking about. After reviewing the past few years of filing history, he said, "Don, how long does it take to fill out this IRS Form 940?" Don said about two hours total, including gathering the information. He continued, "Does it take the same amount of time if you do it the week after the quarter ends as it does the day before it is due?" Of course, the answer was "yes." Then Paul said he had noticed a few errors in some filings. He said he knew Don was capable of correctly calculating the numbers and filing out the forms but it just looked careless, like he was in a hurry and had made silly mistakes.

Paul smiled in a friendly way. He finished with, "Here's the thing. It takes you two hours to do, no matter when you do it. You are behind in some work now and there will always be time challenges in the future. Let's agree to this. I'll help you get caught up on all filings due in the next thirty days and from then on, you do all the reports well ahead of the deadlines. Let's shoot for two weeks ahead but maybe some will be more. Just not less. I promise it will improve the accuracy of the filings and decrease the stress that you feel. It's the same amount of time." Then, as if almost answering the unasked question in the room, he added, "Even if it just sits on your desk for two or three weeks, let's just do it early."

There it was. A simply put, completely logical solution. And in both its simplicity and logic, it was undeniable that Don would accept this and perform as he should. It was confirmed later that day when Don poked his head in my office and admitted that he felt bad and that Paul was right. He would get caught up and not let this happen again.

Don missed a few deadlines in the future, but they were rare. I also saw him change other, related habits. He was more consistent in being prepared for other assignments, especially anytime he was given reasonable notice beforehand. I also think I detected a reduced stress level. There were less frenetic looks from him on busy days and fewer fast walks up and down the hall.

What I remember even more about this story was its impact on me. It wasn't so much on my timeliness of filing reports. It was more about executing *all* kinds of work. Letters that needed to be written, quotes that needed to be sent out, budget preparation and financial reviews, almost everything I did was influenced. It often allowed me time to reflect on a decision I was about to make or the wording I would use. It gave me the extra cushion to review important items and think about their impact without a looming deadline.

I haven't always utilized the "just do it early" theory, just as Don has missed a few deadlines after our talk. However, the concept of having adequate and quality time to consider import-ant matters made a difference in the success of many decisions I made throughout my career.

Ross—"We All Just Want a Quiet Life"

Ross was the vice president of engineering and technical services for a very large concrete contractor. His company was a huge buyer of concrete in our market area, probably the biggest in most years. Having been part of part of my industry for decades, he was hired by this particular contractor to help manage the many aspects of concrete in their construction work.

For an engineer, Ross was very social and charismatic. (Sorry for the stereotype, engineers.) He had a swagger about him and talked louder than others in meetings, especially when he had a point to make. His thoroughly English accent didn't hurt either. He was a hearty drinker and loved to flirt after hours. (Given that this was years ago, the word "flirt" is an understatement. You get the picture.)

My relationship with Ross evolved over the years. On average, we would see each other in meetings a few times a year. Some meetings were perfunctory, reviewing specifications or work scope on a project. Others involved issues with concrete we made for his project or how he handled the concrete we delivered. In other words, it was often about whether he or I was the cause of the problem.

We clashed more than a few times. Early on, we probably didn't think much of each other. As time went by, and we had more opportunities to work together, our mutual respect grew. We were both smarter than we gave each other credit for. My improved appreciation for Ross started on a particularly contentious project.

Ross's company had been hired to do paving at a major Ohio airport. In turn, we were hired by them to supply the concrete. Placing runways, ramps, and aprons at an airport is not a typical matter of compliance with specifications. Not only were they demanding, but the schedule was very tight. The project had to be done in a very short period of time in order not to affect airport operations.

We were called to a meeting to discuss a problem with some of the placed concrete. It wasn't a specific defect but a general pavement quality issue that was being questioned. Ross and I had discussed the issue beforehand and agreed we were both following specifications, but the finished product was less than ideal. We had to explain this to the airport owner, the general contractor we both worked for, and (worst of all) the FAA engineer overseeing the project. The usual plan was for Ross to take the lead and I would add comments as needed or requested.

The meeting started out poorly. The FAA engineer accused everyone but himself of causing the problem. He threatened to reject the pavement and have it torn out if we didn't improve future pavement quality. My first reaction was to defend our performance vigorously; the FAA engineer and his specifications surely were the real culprit. Ross was more diplomatic. He took everyone through the specifications and how it led to the less-than-ideal pavement. He emphasized that we were in compliance and that the specifications should be modified to improve the pavement. I was impressed, but the FAA engineer wasn't.

After some back and forth, a stalemate seemed imminent. The problem was that the FAA wins all "draws" because, ultimately, they would never back down. A stalemate doesn't happen in construction; it just gets broken by the guy with the biggest stick. The meeting took a break and Ross and I huddled in a backroom.

Ross was uncharacteristically quiet and then said to me, "Look mate, this prick has us by the shorthairs, even if we are right. You know we can make the change he asked for and go on with it. What do you think?" I protested. Such a change would cost both of us significant money—almost a quarter of our profit for the project. I told Ross I knew we were right and should fight on. "Can't we take this up the ladder and over his head? He's just wrong. Why should that cost me so much money?!"

Ross paused but was nodding his head in agreement. He looked me straight in the eye and said "Jim," which sounded like "jam" when he said it, "You know what this guy wants? He just wants a quiet life. He doesn't want his superiors showing up one day and questioning the pavement. He doesn't want the bloody mess it will be to modify the specs and get it approved by his bosses. And he doesn't want to spend any more time screwing with me or you. You'd like a quiet life, right? Well, that's all he wants. He wants a quiet life."

He went on to make valid points. The FAA was bigger than both of us, and we want as good a reputation with them as we can get. He explained it was more about the long haul and the future projects at this airport and with the FAA at other airports. Ross knew we could never be "right" and not lose the battle. In the end, we both took a hit on profitability for this project but lived to fight another day. It made more and more sense as time went by. The project was completed to accolades because we both had worked hard to give the airport and the FAA what they wanted.

I learned to take this lesson with me on many other occasions. When we had to deal with customers' issues, it wasn't that I always caved in. It was just that I learned to think more clearly and fully through issues that can cause a customer severe heartburn. Anxiety and stress in your customer can quickly be transferred to you, and those costs may be much higher than giving him a quiet life.

Years later, Ross and I were called in to help solve a problem for the same contractor. They were in the early phases of constructing a manufacturing plant in Tennessee—one of the largest

U.S. investments ever made by a German company. Ross had since retired but was consulting occasionally. I wasn't involved in the project at all until the call came. Essentially, the contractor was being supplied concrete by a local company, but they were experiencing a rash of rejections due to faulty concrete.

Ross and I flew down for a series of meetings over an entire day to discuss the issue. We quickly came to the same conclusion and, after talking between ourselves, recommended a plan of action to solve their issues. It was classic Ross. Our plan would make sure the owner would have a quiet life by utilizing our bullet-proof strategy. Over the course of the next several weeks, it became clear that our plan was correct, but the local company was incapable of executing it. My company was asked to take over the project and we completed the remaining 80 percent of the project at a very handsome profit.

I don't think we would have had the opportunity to complete this project if not for the relationship I had developed with Ross and understanding how to solve problems via lessening the owner's pain threshold. We solved a quality and production issue for this project, but our success was all rooted in service.

Bruce—"The Answer to a Customer's Request Is Always 'Yes' Unless..."

Many years before I joined a formal peer group to help and advise me, I attempted to form my own. It was a group of like-minded executives that meet a couple times a year to discuss best practices and other issues. We also decided to travel, visiting other companies in our industry to try to learn from them. It was a fun and interesting adventure where I made some lifelong friends.

We visited a company in California that had just won the Malcolm Baldrige National Quality Award. This is given annually by the President of the United States to companies that demonstrate quality and performance excellence. This prestigious award had never been awarded to a company in our industry. I had read about this company, and the award, and was curious to learn more.

We flew to California, toured the facility, and got to meet several senior managers. We especially enjoyed our time with Bruce, their CEO. He was a family member of the owners of this multi-generational company but had come from the high-tech industry. It was clear he had different ideas than our industry leaders typically had about running a company.

As the leader of our little group, I spoke with Bruce several times before we met and several times after. He was truly unique; I admired his commitment to the principles they had developed. I didn't agree with everything, but it was hard to deny that Bruce was a visionary. Towards the end of our time there, we had an interesting conversation about customer service. We discussed the challenge of instilling customer service orientation into all employees. Because I could see that every employee of his I met embodied it, I was curious how he did this.

He asked me what I say about customer service to my employees. I told him, "We say the typical things like 'the customer always comes first' or 'we'll do whatever it takes to satisfy a customer' or 'the customer is always right'." I added that I thought everyone understood what these things meant, and we generally provided good service. He probed further and asked, "What do you think those phrases mean? And I'm asking exactly, specifically, what do they mean?" I gave him a long answer, but I wasn't even sure what I said. So, he asked the question a different way, "So, what would your employees say they mean?" I told him the truth. I wasn't sure.

Bruce led me through his own experience with giving clarity on customer service ideals. He said it really boils down to the simple phrase: "If a customer makes a request, the answer is 'yes' unless it is illegal, immoral, unethical, or unsafe." He went on, "It is meant to be simple and memorable. Every employee remembers it because it is written down, and we say it all the time too." It sounded great but I pushed back, "What if it is a crazy request and will cost a ton of money?" Bruce explained the critical piece of this philosophy. He said, "We do it if it is not illegal, immoral, unethical, or unsafe. What I didn't say was what we charge. I want every employee to be authorized to answer a customer's requests, but I only want our sales department or senior management to determine what we will charge for that request. It makes it easy on the employees, but sales or management still has the say in what we charge. Ultimately, the pricing thing takes care of the crazy thing."

Bruce found a way to free most of his employees from even thinking about what they would do for a customer. It gave them a clear and concise way of thinking about customer service. The pricing part prevented mayhem from occurring. I asked Bruce if I could borrow his phrase. He agreed, and I have used it in my own company ever since.

I still love the way our employees embrace this philosophy.

Being able to define something in absolute terms is rare but effective. I also appreciate that our company's reputation has flourished with this concept. Customers knew we would (and almost always could) do whatever they asked. It made us their "Go-To" supplier of choice. It also became the foundation of much of our customer service attitude and character.

Some memorable business lessons have had an impact, but not for their positive spin:

Will—"I Always Make Sure We Have Plausible Deniability"

I was on a golf trip with one of my best customers. We had played golf and were relaxing before dinner. Alcohol had flowed freely throughout the day and there were lots of laughs and storytelling. I had known these guys for many years. They were among my first customers when I started my own company.

Their business had always been challenging. They were tough negotiators, and I seemed to always be giving in more than I wanted to. Despite this, I had stayed with them, mostly because their volume of business would have been hard to replace. Eventually, I replaced their largest supplier and became their primary supplier and was their supplier of choice. This meant that I had opportunities to do their work if I wanted, through matching prices and getting inside information. I thought I was the favored son, and, on these trips, I had access to their top three managers.

As evening approached, the discussion turned to business, as it always did. They talked about how a certain project in another market was going. As I listened and the conversation continued, they were quite candid—as if I were one of them. At one point, they revealed a problem they were having and asked my opinion, since it dealt with concrete. I listened, eager to help and weigh in and to show I was part of the team.

The problem was between them and their supplier—a company just like mine with a good reputation. They described the point of contention and, when they were done, one looked at me and asked how I would handle the situation. I had been following along closely and thought I knew the answer. I said, "I know you may not like this, but it sounds like your own project management really caused the problem. I'd say you probably owe them for the repairs needed but that would only be confirmed by your project manager acknowledging the schedule delay details. It sounds like you know what he did."

They all laughed and congratulated me on my analysis. As the laughter died down, Will, the one closest to that project, said, "You may be right but that's only because you now know everything we do. That supplier doesn't. We always maintain 'plausible deniability'." That brought an even heartier laugh from the three and I even chuckled a bit. Will went further, in case I didn't understand their crucial business philosophy. "Jimmy, they don't know everything we do, and they don't need to know everything we do. They are the supplier and we are the customer. Things happen and we deal with them. The point is that we may or may not be responsible for the problem, but we are always going to maintain plausible deniability. That way, we can say that we don't know, or we are not sure, or we don't have all the facts. It's essentially true or at least plausible. Get it?"

There was more laughter, and I smiled and nodded that I understood. We broke up to get ready for dinner and the subject wasn't brought up again. However, I kept replaying the conversation in my head for the next few weeks. It made me think of a lesson I learned as a teenager and still see happening today. We've all had a friend or relative quietly say, "I swore I wouldn't tell anyone, but listen to what I just heard from so-and-so," and then some secret comes out—a secret they shouldn't share and you may not want to know. We've all experienced such cringeworthy moments. It teaches us an important lesson, namely, don't share anything with that person. They can't keep a secret. They will betray you as they just did their other friend.

What I learned from that conversation with my best customer—comparing them to the secret-sharer—was that they do this kind of thing regularly. It is part of who they are and someday, eventually, they would surely do it to me. I wasn't part of their company, and they only let me in their circle for short times such as during an alcohol-fueled golf trip.

Afterwards, I never said anything to them about it. I simply raised my guard and kept my eyes and ears open when we did projects with them. It was easy to get lulled into thinking that such "good friends" and "good customers" wouldn't perpetrate some untoward act, but I kept on my toes.

Years later, when I had almost forgotten the incident, we had a very difficult issue on one of their projects. There were several accounts of what happened from our respective employees, but the facts seemed straightforward. As we slowly worked toward a resolution, I finally got my taste of their "plausible deniability." It was something less than a spoken, boldfaced lie, but it was close enough. I knew I'd been had.

The incident was the beginning of the end with this customer. We intentionally did less and less work with them
until it was all but not nonexistent. I knew I could never
trust them fully or this would just happen repeatedly. While
I was aware of their unethical potential after the golf trip,
I did not act fast enough to get away from them. It was
seductive relationship due to the size of the sales volume
but nonetheless one I did not want and would not endure.

I pride myself on being intuitive and able to read people well. I
think I was dead-on accurate with these guys. I just didn't act quickly
or proactively enough to limit the damage they would cause.

Tom—"Fair" and "Tell Me What You Just Heard"

In the middle of the difficult issue in the above story, I had a series of
meetings with Tom, that company's CEO. It was an attempt on my
part to resolve the issue as discussions and progress stalled with his #2
and #3 guys. We made some progress, but it was small and incremental. Overall, I could not overcome their basic ethical shortcomings.

In one of the meetings, I meticulously laid out the facts I knew
about the issue. Tom had a cursory knowledge of it and listened
while I presented background and took him through the logical
course of events. It was a case of mutual mistakes where we had
made the first one, but they made the final and fateful one. In the
end, the issue would not have arisen if not for our mistake, but
they had compounded it many times over.

I ended my monologue with a comment about what would be a fair outcome. I was not running from our initial mistake but merely trying to own it and balance the overall costs to be shouldered from the episode. I told Tom, "I've been honest about our mistake and how it affected this problem. We will take every bit of blame due us and more. I just can't agree with Will's assessment that it is entirely ours. He knows that too. It's not even close to fair."

Tom looked at me like I was a child. He cut in and said, "Jim, you know what 'fair' is? It's where you get cotton candy and ride the Ferris wheel. It doesn't have anything to do with how we are going to resolve this." I stared at him as he continued, "I told this same thing to my fourteen-year-old son a few weeks ago. He was complaining about some bullshit and how I wasn't fair. Guess what? Life's not fair. You want fair then go to the fair and eat some cotton candy, but this is real life and the real business world, and you're just going to have to pony up on this one."

I always thought Tom was very smart and seemed like a good guy in general. Now, I was seeing limitations to his character. First the laughing agreement about "plausible deniability" and now this. I knew the conversation was over. I left his office to consider my alternatives.

Several months after we had resolved the issue (greatly to their benefit), I chatted with Tom in his office—just a catching up, semi-social, and impromptu encounter. As usual, he was interesting and engaging, but I noticed more of the true character coming out, which I would probably have dismissed before. After a few pleasantries, he launched into a new philosophy he had read about in a business book and how he was using it to change how his company managed relationships with suppliers such as me. Half-way into this mini-lecture, I was trying to figure how to get the hell out of there.

After he was done and I had heard and digested every word, he looked at me for a second as if waiting for a response. I didn't say anything. The less said and the less I engaged, the sooner I am on my way. So, he said, "Tell me what you just heard." I looked at him and cocked my head inquisitively. He repeated, "Tell me what you just heard. Tell me what I just said." I had had enough. I was polite but said, "I'm not sure what you mean but I heard your new supplier philosophy." I stood up and said, "Good luck with that. Seems like you've thought that through." We shook hands and I smiled—not letting on that I was definitely being facetious.

Later, I learned from members of his Board of Directors that he had recently begun employing that same comment with them. They were equally taken aback and even upset.

In the media, there are frequent debates about whether "words matter." I am now firmly on the side of "words *do* matter." It matters what is said and how it is said. In many cases, it leads to behavior modeled perfectly by the words. This was a prime example. It was also a prime example of how arrogance can get the better of people. Misplaced confidence and an attitude of superiority are never appreciated. The smartest people I have ever met exuded confidence but never arrogance. If nothing else, they embodied humility and were always unpretentious.

CONCLUSION

AT THE END OF THE DAY

It has been just over two years since I sold my business. I've been as busy as ever, just with a lot of different things that are unlike running a company day in and day out. Here is a rundown.

Right After Closing

I spent about four hours in my attorney's office on closing day. Closing transactions aren't like they used to be. There is no assembly of attorneys and sellers and buyers in a conference room. There was just me, him, and a few associates coming in and out. We were in his largest conference room, which could have seated over twenty people around a huge wood table. Spaced about a foot apart and ringing the entire table were small stacks of paper. Each stack was only a page or two. Eventually, my attorney, Dave, said

229

to begin signing. I assumed somewhere, in the buyer's attorney's office, the same thing was happening.

I sat down, read the first page in a stack, and signed it. I did the same with the next, and the next, and about an hour later I was back where I started and had signed my name a few dozen times. Now, I waited for Dave who was coming in and out. There were more documents to sign, some new, and some reworked from ones I had signed before. Towards the end, it was often just me in that big conference room, staring at all the papers I'd signed.

Finally, I had signed everything needed, and Dave and I shook hands. He said the other side had notified him that the wiring of funds would start immediately. A handful of miscellaneous payments to banks and then one large one to me.

On and off, for the rest of the day, I checked my bank account, waiting for the wire. Dave and the investment banker reported that all wires had gone out. Still nothing in my account. By the end of the day, it still wasn't there. Saturday, it wasn't there. I called the bank president and he checked. Nothing. "It'll probably show up Monday," he said. Monday?! No one else knew anything and the wire was reported as sent. Nothing to do but wait.

Monday morning finally came, and the wire showed up. No one ever could explain what happened. The buyer's attorney had a printed confirmation that it went out Friday. It just didn't come in until Monday to my bank. While I had assurances from everyone not to worry, the celebration was a little subdued over the weekend at my house—an oddly anti-climactic ending!

The New Owner

The new owner and I had several conversations about my coming to work for him. We talked about me running my old company rolled up with their other acquisitions in the region. They also had plans for more acquisitions in the coming months.

Although the conversations were interesting, neither he nor I felt this would be a good fit. We were both successful but had different philosophies about running a business and different ideas about culture. I know there was healthy, mutual respect, but not much in common. We never pursued formal discussions, which worked out best for both of us.

My Employees

As part of the negotiations to sell my company, the buyer agreed to hire every one of my employees and honor both their current pay and match or exceed their benefits. That included honoring their years of service and carrying it over to their company. It especially made a difference in vacation time.

Most everyone stayed on initially. Over the first year, a few left, but for the most part, people stayed and worked just as they had before. I came into the office almost every day for three or four months after the sale, in part to wind down my old corporations and in part to offer support to my former employees. I'm not sure I contributed much to the business itself, but I felt a sense of duty to make sure the transition was as smooth and seamless as possible. This was mostly for my people but also for the new owner.

I think the transition was harder for some, but everyone was professional and continued to give their all for the new owner. I was proud of them. They were still working hard and doing the right thing as they learned new "ropes" and became accustomed to new bosses and ways of doing things.

Investing the Proceeds

About six months before closing, even before we had agreed to terms with the buyer, I had begun to talk to different investment advisors. I had done most of my own investing with online accounts up to then, but I knew I wanted professional help when I sold my company.

I met my current investment team by way of introduction from a business broker. The introduction led to several meetings, emails, and phone calls with John Hahn at Goldman Sachs, who has been my trusted advisor ever since. (Although this sounds like a plug for John and Goldman Sachs, it is mostly a suggestion to seek out this kind of relationship well before closing.)

John and his team were helpful in many ways before I ever sent them a dime. This included ideas on structuring the sale of my business and, most importantly, on minimizing taxes. It also helped that much of this work, and pre-work, for investments was done without time pressures or distractions in the months before the sale. Getting them involved early made a big difference.

Winding Down the Corporations

While I keep referring to selling my company, it was actually the sale of assets from three different corporations. An asset sale meant that I kept the corporate entities and then had to wind them down. This included the usual paying of outstanding invoices and filing of many returns.

While I was literate in terms of reporting and filings, I did not do much, if any of it myself. My controller filed most of these and some (such as payroll filings) were done by third parties. However, I still found myself dealing with a lot of filing and tax matters over the next two years. It has been a slow and steady drip—and a pain in the rear.

If I had to do it over again, I would have done a better job of listing and tracking everything that needed to be done and then seeing it through. A little help from outside accountants and attorneys would probably have saved time and money as well.

New Job(s)?

When the news of my company's sale went public, I started getting calls from people in my industry. Some were inquiries about whether I would consult on a matter or issue they had. I always listened but rarely ended up doing any consulting work. Most of the time, the request was for a specific area that I felt was better handled by a consultant already working in that space. For these, I would pass along the information of an expert that I knew could help them. At other times, requests involved strategic business issues or questions. There, I would take on work where I felt I could be of real value. It wasn't that I had decided to be a consultant but only that they were friends and I wanted to help. I did so with one major condition. I never charged or accepted anything—other than bottles of wine!

I talked to a few private equity firms. Two were referrals from friends. I spent some time looking at potential acquisitions with them but never participated in any deals. Two others ended up being a series of discussions about possibly investing in industries that I have expertise in. These were interesting conversations, but nothing arose from them. I may not be a great match for private equity. So much of my thinking revolves around building value, and particularly long-term value, while PE firms always look to flip their acquisitions within short timeframes.

I have also had several inquiries about working for other companies. There have been a few CEO inquiries and a few COO inquiries but nothing that fit. I was not necessarily looking for a job but some of these have been interesting. One thing they all had in common was that I would not be the owner and, therefore, report to someone or a board. While I am not opposed to the idea, I decided that to work for someone else, even as CEO, would require a huge comfort level with that person or group. Fortunately, that is a luxury I can afford.

What I Didn't Do

Despite many friends asking me these questions, I didn't do any of the following:

» Buy a new car: I drive the same one as the day I sold the company, with 125,000 miles and counting. Maybe I should buy one?
» Play more golf: I still don't have enough time to do this more. Currently about six times per year is my max!

- » Take vacations: We've taken two in two years, each less than a week. We would like to take a few more!
- » Change our lifestyle: Same restaurants, same clothes, same everything.
- » Sleep in: I still get up at the same time each morning.

My wife and I lived a nice life before I sold the company, and we are happy with it today. To change much about our lifestyles would not make us any happier. I also think it's important to not change your lifestyle or habits suddenly or dramatically. The common denominator then and now is trying to find more time to do what's important.

What I Did Do

We did buy some land and are building a new house on it. This only partially counts as a big change. We had been looking for a small farm for our horses for a while before I sold. We just happened to find this farm in the summer after I sold the business. It also means that I am a farmer now. We have about thirty acres of hay that is cut and baled three to four times a year and another thirty acres of pasture for the horses.

We also have invested in my wife's career. After spending much of her time helping others in personal coaching and professional development, she has started a more intentional approach to reach beyond her one-on-one interactions and offer a wider audience access to her expertise. She can be found here: www.trishmckinnley.com.

Writing This Book

Writing this book grew out of conversations with my wife, friends, and some business associates. There was some cajoling and encouragement but mostly it came down to whether I had something unique to say that could help my fellow small business owners. When I started writing, it flowed out easily and took on a life of its own. It became something I had to do. I hope it's been an interesting read and you found it valuable for your own business.

ABOUT THE AUTHOR

Successful entrepreneur Jim Spurlino is the founder of Spurlino Materials, a supplier of construction materials. During his college years, he worked full-time for a privately owned construction materials company. After graduating, Jim quickly rose through its ranks and became vice president and general manager before the age of thirty. Soon after, he started his own company with a personal investment of $40,000 and lots of hard work. He built a business that began with a local reputation for quality products and excellent service into a firm that was nationally recognized. The company's notable achievements included supplying concrete for the Bristol Motor Speedway and the Indianapolis Colts stadium. After seventeen years, Jim realized the full value of his efforts when he sold his company for $30 million—not a bad return.